1001 Teaching Props

Simple Props to Make for Working With Young Children

Warren Publishing House
Everett, WA

Compiled by
The Totline Staff

Some of the activity ideas in this book were originally contributed by *Totline Newsletter* subscribers. We wish to acknowledge Catherine Abraham, Geneva, IL; Bettie Adams, Omaha, NE; Betty Ruth Baker, Waco, TX; Denise Bedell, Westland, MI; Sr. Mary Bezold, Melbourne, KY; Lisa M.Blum, Del Rio, TX; Ricke A. Bly, Tyler, MN; Janice Bodenstedt, Jackson, MI; Kim Bohl, Adrian, MI; Karen Brown, Siloam Springs, AR; Tamara Clohessy, Eureka, CA; Kit Cooper, Pittsfield, MA; Sarah Cooper, Arlington, TX; June Crow, Weaverville, NC; Joyce DeVilbiss, Silver Springs, MD; Cindy Dingwall, Palatine, IL; Elisabetta, DiStravolo,West Reading, PA; Ruth Engle, Kirkland, WA; Jeanne Feola, Verona, NY; Karen Focht, Reading, PA; Rita Galloway, Harlingen, TX; Connie Gillilan, Hardy, NE; Joan Giorgi, Massena, NY; Lanette L. Guttierrez, Olympia, WA; Diane Himplemann, Ringwood, IL; Colraine Pettipaw Hunley, Doylestown, PA; Joan Hunter, Elbridge, NY; Barbara H. Jackson, Denton, TX; Ellen Javernick, Loveland, CO; Sr. Linda Kaman, RSM, Pittsburgh, PA; Barbara Kingsley, Flushing, NY; Judy Lahore, Seattle, WA; Debra Lindahl, Libertyville, IL; Cathy Lorenz, Mountlake Terrace, WA; Marilyn Dias Machosky, Westerville, OH; Donna L. Maille, Fair Haven, NJ; Barb Mazzochi, Villa Park, IL; Judith McNitt, Adrian, MI; Rose C. Merenda, Warwick, RI; Susan A. Miller, Kutztown, PA; Linda Moenck, Webster City, IA; Donna Mullennix, Thousand Oaks, CA; Susan M. Paprocki, Northbrook, IL; Dawn Picolelli, Wilmington, DE; Maxine E. Pincott, Windsor, CT; Ruth Prall, Sterling, CO; Lois E. Putnam, Pilot Mountain, NC; Heather Ray, Downingtown, PA; Mame Reback, Kenmore, NY; Jane Roake, Oswego, IL; Barbara Robinson, Glendale, AZ; Deborah A. Roessel, Flemington, NJ; Susan Schoelkopf, Rochester, WA; Karen Seehusan, Fort Dodge, IA; Vicki Shannon, Napton, MD; Betty Silkunas, Lansdale, PA; Leslie Wagner, Fredonia, NY; Kristine Wagoner, Puyallup, WA; Marie Wheeler, Tacoma, WA; Betty Loew White, South Beechwold, OH; Nancy C. Windes, Denver, CO; Saundra Winnett, Lewisville, TX; Peggy Wolf, Pittsburgh, PA.

Editorial Staff: Gayle Bittinger, Kathleen Cubley, Brenda Lalonde,
Elizabeth McKinnon, Susan M. Sexton, Jean Warren, Erica West
Production Staff:
Manager: Eileen Carbary; *Assistant:* Jo Anna Brock
Book and Cover Design: Kathy Kotomaimoce
Computer Graphics: Carol DeBolt, Sarah Ness, Eric Stovall
Illustrated by: Gary Mohrmann

ISBN 0-911019-46-4

Library of Congress Catalog Card Number 91-65931
Printed in the United States of America
Published by: Warren Publishing House
P.O. Box 2250
Everett, WA 98203

20 19 18 17 16 15 14 13 12 11 10 9 8 7 6 5

Introduction

Let's face it — teaching comes alive when we can develop our own learning materials. So at Totline, we have put together this book of props, each of which can be made easily and inexpensively.

1001 Teaching Props is a collection of the best teaching props found in Totline publications over the last 10 years, plus hundreds of new prop ideas compiled by the Totline staff.

On the following pages you will find suggestions for making art props, holiday props, learning games, movement props, puppets, science props, water toys and more.

Arranged in dictionary format, *1001 Teaching Props* is really an instant resouce guide with the props listed alphabetically. In addition, there is a materials index at the end of the book for those times when a box of craft sticks or a stack of paper cups appears and you want ideas for things to make with them.

The Multi-Usable Learning Game props were taken from our book, *Teaching Toys*, which is now out of print.

Totline books are known for their appropriateness and readability. We hope you will find *1001 Teaching Props* to be another useful and easy-to-use teaching guide.

Contents

Contents

Art Props

Art Displays

1 Burlap Banner

Cut a piece of burlap to the desired size. Pull several strings on one end of the burlap to create a fringe. Lay a dowel on the opposite end, fold the burlap over the dowel and glue or sew the burlap in place. Tie a piece of yarn to the ends of the dowel to make a hanger. If desired, secure the yarn with glue. Use the banner as a background and pin the children's artwork to it.

2 Display Strips

Attach bulletin board strips made out of corkboard to walls. The strips use little space and can accommodate numerous pieces of artwork. Purchase them or make your own by cutting corkboard into 4-inch-wide strips. Attach the strips to one wall or to several walls around the room. Use push pins to hang the children's artwork from the strips.

3 Display Tree

Cut a large tree shape out of brown construction paper. If desired, laminate it or cover it with clear self-stick paper for durability. Attach the tree to a wall or a bulletin board and hang the children's artwork from its branches.

4 Jump Rope Display

Stretch a multi-colored jump rope between two poles, along a wall or across a door opening. Use clothespins to hang paintings or other artwork from the jump rope to create a colorful display.

5 Magnetic Clips

Put large clips with magnets attached on a refrigerator door or other metallic surface. Hang children's artwork from the clips.

6 Metal Clips

Screw metal clips into the wall at the children's eye level. Personalize each clip by writing a child's name on it with a permanent felt-tip marker. Then let each child choose a picture to be displayed from his or her clip. Let the children decide when to change their pictures.

7 Sheet Display

Make a simple display using a white or light-colored flat bed sheet. Hang the sheet on a wall and attach the children's artwork to the sheet with pins or tape.

8 Three-Dimensional Art Display

Fasten small cardboard boxes to bulletin boards to display three-dimensional artwork.

9 Window Shade

Hang artwork from a window shade that remains drawn.

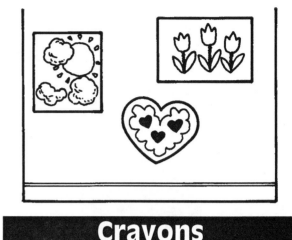

Crayons

10 Colorful Crayon Rounds

Chop a variety of old peeled crayons into ¼-inch pieces and place them in the baking cups of an old muffin tin. Heat the crayons at 250 degrees for 5 minutes or until the crayon pieces just begin to melt together. Turn off the oven and leave the muffin tin in it. Allow the crayons to cool in the oven before removing them from the muffin tin. The colorful crayon rounds are ready to use.

11 | Cookie Sheet Coloring Board

Cut a piece of paper to fit inside a cookie sheet with raised edges. Place the paper in the cookie sheet and give it and some crayons to a child. Let the child color on the paper while it is in the cookie sheet. This helps keep the child from making crayon marks on the table or other surface.

12 | Crayon Storage

Store crayons in wide-mouth containers according to color: all yellow crayons in one container, all red crayons in another container, etc. Then use the containers for color-matching games when your children are putting crayons away after art projects.

13 | Rainbow Crayons

For each child tape two or three different colors of crayons together to make a rainbow crayon. Let the children use the crayons for drawing. Show them how to use the rainbow crayons to draw rainbow arcs.

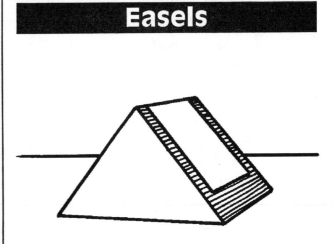

14 | Box Easel

Select a sturdy cardboard box. Cut off the top flaps or remove the lid. Then cut the box in half diagonally. (See illustration.) Discard the top half of the box. Set the remaining half on a table like a tent. Tape paper to one or both sides of the box easel.

15 | Wall Easel

Attach clips to a piece of laminated board (available at home and garden stores). Nail a 4-inch-wide strip of wood to the bottom of the board to hold paint containers. Hang the board on a wall at the children's eye level. The laminated board makes paint cleanup easy.

Paint Storage

16 Aluminum Pie Pans
Pour paint into aluminum pie pans. The pans are especially good for holding paint for printing projects.

17 Baby Food Jars
Use baby food jars with lids as paint containers at an easel.

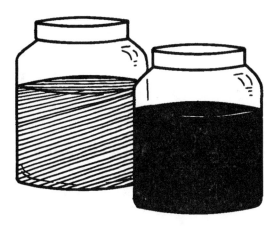

18 Dishwashing Liquid Bottles
Store tempera paints in dishwashing liquid bottles. The paint can then be squirted into paint dishes or cups, even by the children.

19 Egg Carton Sections
Cut egg cartons into long sections to use as paint containers at an easel.

20 Egg Cartons

Egg cartons make handy paint containers when the children are painting with cotton swabs. Cut the cartons in thirds to make four-part containers and pour small amounts of paint into the cups.

21 Frosting Containers
Ready-made cake frosting containers make good paint holders for the easel, and their lids will prevent the paint from drying out.

22 Frozen Food Trays
Frozen food trays are good disposable paint holders, especially those with sections to hold more than one color.

23 Glue Bottles

Cut down on paint drips by storing liquid tempera paint in empty glue bottles. Any amount of paint can then be squirted quickly and neatly into paint pans.

24 Milk Carton Holder

To prevent paint cups from tipping over when the children are painting with brushes, make a cup holder from an empty milk carton. Cut holes along the length of the carton and pop in your paint cups.

25 Muffin Tins

Muffin tins make excellent containers for paint projects when several different colors are needed.

26 Paint Container Holder

When using baby food jars as paint containers, make a holder for them by cutting holes out of the lid of an egg carton.

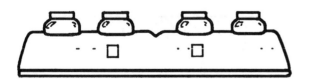

27 Paint Jar Tote

Put baby food jars filled with paint in an empty six-pack soft-drink bottle carton that has a handle. The carton can serve as a tote as well as a paint container holder.

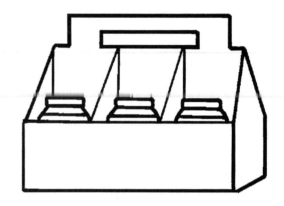

28 Peanut Butter Jars

Use small plastic peanut butter jars for paint containers. They have wide mouths and won't tip over easily.

29 Plastic Cups

Sturdy plastic cups in 4- or 6-ounce sizes make great paint containers. They also have lids which can be resealed to keep the paint from drying out.

30 Plastic Foam Trays

Pour small amounts of paint into plastic foam food trays for disposable paint holders.

31 Plastic Utility Tote

Put paint containers in a plastic utility tote to prevent them from tipping over. Use the tote when painting at tables or on the floor.

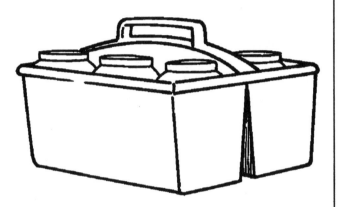

32 Sponge Holders

To keep paint jars from tipping over while being used on a table, make holders out of sponges. Cut a hole the size of each jar in the center of each sponge, then fit the jars in the holes. Besides keeping the paint jars upright, the sponges will also catch drips.

33 Yogurt Containers

Store tempera paint in yogurt containers for use at an easel. The lids will keep the paint from drying out between uses.

Paintbrushes

34 Feathers

Give the children large sheets of construction paper. Set out different colors of tempera paint and long feathers. Let the children dip the feathers into the paint and use them like brushes.

35 Paintbrush Alternatives

Let the children paint with any of the following items:

- cotton balls
- cotton swabs
- craft sticks
- evergreen twigs
- pastry brushes
- sponges

36 Roller-Top Bottles

Pry the roller tops off of empty deodorant containers. Wash the tops and the bottles thoroughly and allow them to dry. Then fill the bottles with different colors of liquid tempera paint and replace the roller tops. Let the children use the bottles to draw lines, shapes or letters on sheets of construction paper.

37 Shoe Polish Bottles

Pry the foam applicator tops off of empty sponge applicator shoe polish bottles. Wash the bottles and applicators thoroughly. Refill the bottles with diluted tempera paint and replace the applicators.

38 Squeeze Bottles

Collect plastic squeeze-type condiment bottles (the kind used for mustard and ketchup). Fill the bottles with different colors of extra-thick tempera paint. Let the children squeeze the paint on large pieces of construction paper or butcher paper to create lines, shapes or letters.

Printing Props

39 Balloons

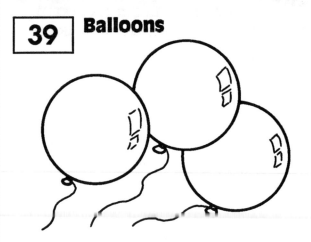

Partially blow up several small balloons. Let the children dip the balloons into tempera paints then press them onto sheets of white construction paper to create balloon prints.

40 Balls

Set out several different kinds of small balls such as foam balls, tennis balls and rubber balls. Have the children dip the balls into tempera paint and then press them onto pieces of construction paper. Let them try making prints with each type of ball.

41 Berry Baskets

Have the children dip the bottoms of plastic berry baskets into tempera paint, then press them on construction paper to make designs.

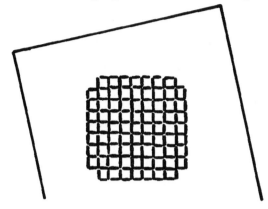

42 Blocks

Collect a variety of small blocks in different sizes and shapes. Give the children pieces of construction paper and the blocks. Let them dip the blocks into paint and then press them on their papers to make prints.

43 Cookie Cutters

Let the children use cookie cutters dipped in tempera paint to make prints.

44 Corncobs

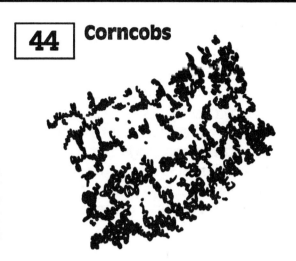

Peel the husks off corncobs. Allow the cobs to dry overnight. Let the children roll the cobs on paint pads and then roll the cobs across pieces of construction paper to make prints. Or let the children make prints with the ends of the corncobs.

45 Gadgets

Let the children print with a variety of kitchen gadgets. Try such gadgets as a potato masher, a tart pan, a funnel, a spatula or a wooden meat tenderizer.

46 Household Items

Give the children such household items as corks, small wood scraps, plastic foam pieces or cardboard tubes to use for printing.

47 Lids

Collect metal jar lids in a variety of sizes. Make a handle for the top of each lid by setting a small piece of wood on a flat surface, placing the lid upside down on top of it and nailing the lid and wood together. Let the children pick up the lids by the handles, dip them into paint and then press them on pieces of paper to make prints.

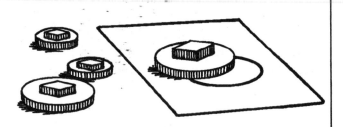

48 Potatoes

Cut potatoes in half. Use a sharp knife to carve designs in the cut ends of the potatoes. Let the children press the potatoes on a paint pad, then on paper.

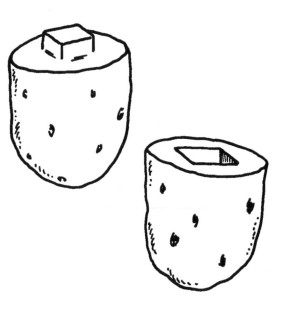

49 Puzzle Pieces

Use commercial foam-rubber puzzle pieces for sponge painting. Let the children dip the pieces into paint and then press them on paper.

50 Rubber Stamps

Invest in an assortment of rubber stamps in animal, flower or toy shapes. Let the children use them year after year for making wrapping paper, greeting cards and cards for matching games, or for stamping designs on watercolor paintings.

Sewing Props

51 Bobby Pin Needles

Let the children use bobby pins for sewing needles. Bobby pins have blunt ends and are stiff, easy to thread, and inexpensive. They can be used for sewing cards, for stringing beads or macaroni or for any project that requires putting string, yarn or thread through holes in paper.

52 Glue Needles

Dip the ends of yarn pieces into glue. Allow the glue to dry. Have the children use the stiff ends of the yarn pieces as needles.

53 Greeting Card Sewing Cards

Punch holes around the edges of greeting cards and let the children sew around them with yarn.

54 Plastic Foam Lacing Shapes

Cut large shapes out of plastic foam food trays. Use a hole punch to punch holes around the outside edges of the shapes. Let the children sew around the shapes with yarn.

55 Plastic Needles

Purchase plastic blunt-ended needles (available at craft and yarn stores). They are safer for the children to use than ordinary needles.

56 Plastic Sewing Cards

Save large plastic laundry detergent bottles. Cut off the tops and bottoms. Cut large simple shapes out of the sides of the bottles. Punch holes around the edges of the shapes with a hole punch. Have the children use yarn or shoe laces to sew around the edges of the shapes.

57 Shoelaces

Use shoelaces for lacing or sewing projects instead of pieces of yarn.

58 Tape Needles

Wrap tape around the ends of yarn pieces to make simple, safe needles.

Smocks

59 Pillowcase Smocks

Old pillowcases make great art smocks that can be tossed into the washing machine after each use. Cut arm and head holes along the pillowcase seams. Then slip the open ends over the children's heads.

60 Shirt Smocks

Use discarded men's shirts for painting smocks. Just cut off the collars and the bottom halves of the sleeves and let the children wear the shirts backwards.

61 Shower Curtain Smocks

Make waterproof smocks out of discarded shower curtains. Cut the curtains into child-sized ovals. Then in the center of the ovals, cut out circles for head holes.

62 Tablecloth Smocks

Use a tablecloth with vinyl on one side and cloth on the other to make smocks for water play, painting and other potentially messy activities. Cut the tablecloth into rectangles. Then near one end of each rectangle, cut out a circle large enough to slip over a child's head.

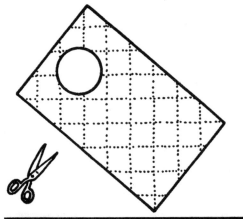

63 Throwaway Smocks

For quick and easy smocks, cut arm and head holes out of plastic trash bags. These are good for extra-messy projects, since they can be thrown out after use.

Weaving Looms

64 Board Loom

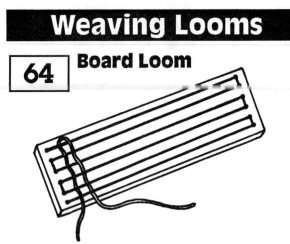

Make a loom by pounding nails into the opposite ends of a piece of board. Wrap yarn around the nails to create a warp. Let the children weave yarn, fabric, feathers or other materials on the board loom.

65 Cardboard Tube Loom

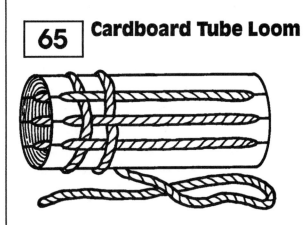

Cut slits in the ends of a cardboard tube. Run yarn lengthwise between the slits to create a warp. (See illustration.) Then let a child weave yarn over and under the warp around the tube.

Chicken Wire Loom

Cut a square from chicken wire that has small holes. Cover the sharp edges with tape. Tie one end of a piece of yarn through one of the holes and tape the other end to make a needle. Show a child how to weave the yarn in and out of the holes in the chicken wire loom.

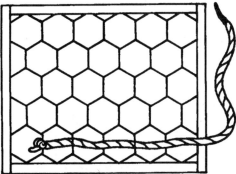

Fish Net Loom

67
Set out a fish net. Give the children long pieces of thick yarn or ribbon. Let them weave their ribbon and yarn pieces over and under the threads of the fish net.

Fork Loom

68
Let a child weave yarn around the tines of a fork.

Plastic Basket Looms

69
Collect a plastic berry basket for each child. Have the children select thin yarn pieces to weave in and out of the holes in their baskets.

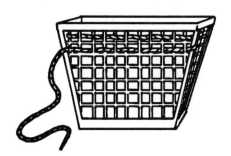

Weaving Trays

70

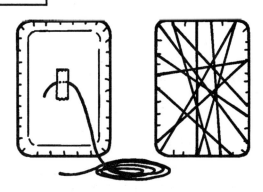

Cut slits around the edges of plastic foam food trays. Cut yarn into manageable lengths and tape one piece to the back of each tray. Let the children wind the yarn around their trays, each time passing it through one of the slits. Encourage them to crisscross their trays in any way they wish to create designs. When the children have finished, trim the ends of the yarn and tape them to the backs of the trays.

More Art Props

Art Dryer

71

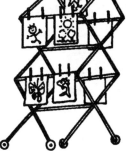

Find a collapsible wooden clothes hanger. Set it up by the art center and let the children attach their finished art projects with clothespins. This allows paintings to dry in a small space.

72 Berry Ink

After mashing various berries (blueberries or blackberries) and straining out their juices, have the children practice writing by dipping toothpicks into the ink and making designs on paper.

73 Easy Stickers

Cut such shapes as circles, triangles, flowers or leaves out of brightly colored self-stick paper. Peel the backing off of the shapes and lightly attach them to waxed paper.

74 Fingerpainting Bag

Pour ⅓ cup fingerpaint into a reclosable plastic bag. Release the air from the bag and seal it. Let a child fingerpaint on top of the bag to make interesting designs without a lot of mess.

75 Glitter Dispensers

For neat glitter dispensers, use plastic bottles with perforated caps, such as spice bottles or bottles that cookie sprinkles come in. These bottles help keep the children's hands cleaner and less glitter will be wasted.

76 Lid Glue Containers

For small craft projects, use gallon milk bottle lids as glue containers. The children won't stick their whole hands into the containers, and there is less mess to clean up afterwards.

77 Mess Catcher

Put an old shower curtain under your work table to catch spills during messy art projects.

78 | Paper Towel Paint Pads

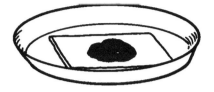

Fold a paper towel in half and place it in a shallow container. Pour a small amount of tempera paint on the towel to make a paint pad.

79 | Plastic Ribbon Art

Cut plastic ribbon into a variety of shapes. Let the children arrange the shapes on a dampened window-pane or mirror to create pictures.

80 | Sponge Paint Pad

Put a thin sponge in a shallow container. Pour a small amount of tempera paint on the sponge to make a paint pad. This paint pad works especially well for printing projects.

81 | Star Cut-Outs

Fold a rectangular piece of paper in half. Then with the folded edge at the bottom, fold the paper as indicated by the arrows and dotted lines in the illustration. Cut through all thicknesses as shown.

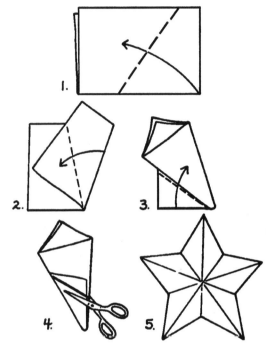

82 | Tablecloth

Spread an old vinyl tablecloth underneath the art table to catch messy spills.

83 | Tub Glue Containers

Use margarine tubs for glue or paste containers. Their lids make for easy storage.

84 | Washcloth Paint Pad

Fold a washcloth in half. Place the washcloth in a shallow container. Pour a small amount of tempera paint on the washcloth to make a paint pad.

Birthday Props

85 Birthday Banner

Write "Good News! (Child's name) is (age) today!" on a classified ads page from a newspaper and hang it on your door.

86 Birthday Box

Fill a box with stickers, felt-tip markers, small toys, pencils and other inexpensive gifts. Decorate the box with birthday giftwrap. On his or her special day, let the birthday child select a gift from the box.

87 Birthday Button

Make a special button that says "Today is my birthday!" or "Birthday Girl/Boy" and let the birthday child wear it.

88 Birthday Card

Mail a handmade birthday card or certificate to the birthday child at his or her home.

89 Birthday Hat

Cut out a 3-inch-wide construction paper strip that is long enough to fit around the birthday child's head. Cut the appropriate number of candle shapes out of different colors of construction paper and add yellow construction paper flames. Glue the candles on the construction paper strip and write "Happy Birthday, (child's name)!" below them. Adjust the hat to fit the child's head and secure it with tape.

90 Birthday Necklace

Cut a ribbon shape out of construction paper as shown. Write "Happy Birthday! Today I am ___ years old!" on it and add the birthday child's name and birthdate. String the ribbon shape on a piece of yarn and put it around the birthday child's neck.

91 Birthday Pennant

Decorate a pennant-shaped piece of construction paper with the birthday child's name, age and birthdate. Add one self-stick star for each year. Attach the pennant to a cardboard tube and let the birthday child take the pennant home.

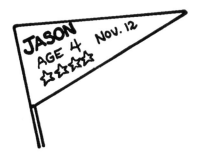

Calendar Markers

92 Candles

Cut candle shapes out of construction paper. Write each child's name on a separate shape. Attach the candles to the dates of the children's birthdays on your calendar.

93 Crowns

Write the children's names and new ages on construction paper crown shapes. Attach the crowns to the appropriate dates on your calendar.

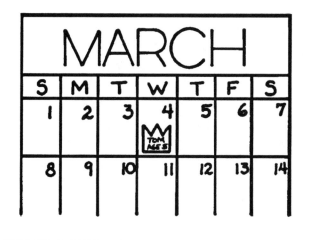

94 Numbers

For each child cut the number of his or her new age out of construction paper, write the child's name on it and attach it to the appropriate date on your calendar.

Room Props

95 Birthday Bag

Put several small objects into a paper bag. Include birthday items such as a birthday candle, a birthday hat and a birthday napkin. Have the children sit in a circle with the birthday child sitting next to you. Let the birthday child reach into the bag and take out an object. Use the object to begin telling a special birthday story. Have the child continue taking one object at a time from the bag. As he or she does so, incorporate the objects into your story.

96 Birthday Chair

Purchase a sturdy wooden chair at a garage sale or a flea market. Clean up the chair, then paint it with bright colors and add the words "Happy Birthday." Let the birthday child have the honor of sitting in the birthday chair on his or her special day.

97 Birthday Play Kit

Make and collect items to create a birthday kit for the children to play with on birthdays. Make a cake from plaster of Paris, placing several plastic birthday candle holders in the top before the plaster sets. Place the plaster cake in a box along with birthday candles (with the wicks cut off), birthday hats and decorated napkins, plates and cups.

98 Birthday Throne

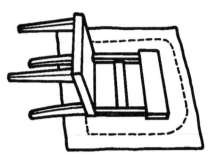

Make a fabric slipcover to turn an ordinary chair into a birthday throne. Place a large piece of paper on the floor and lay the back of a straight-backed chair on it. Trace around the back of the chair, adding 2 inches all the way around it. Then cut out the tracing to make a pattern. Place the pattern on a piece of velour, velveteen or other royal-looking fabric and cut out two pieces. With the right sides of the fabric pieces together, sew around the sides and top, leaving the bottom open. Turn the cover right side out and slip it over the back of the chair to make a birthday throne.

99 Cake And Candles Chair Cover

Make the chair cover as described in prop 98. Glue a birthday cake shape cut from felt to the chair cover. Add a strip of self-gripping fastener to the top of the cake. Cut several candle shapes out of felt and put a small strip of self-gripping fastener on each one. Then let the birthday child add the correct number of felt candles to the cake and sit in his or her special chair.

100 Felt Birthday Cake

Cut a birthday cake shape out of felt and decorate it with felt scraps as desired. Cut several candle shapes out of felt and glue on yellow flame shapes. Place the birthday cake shape on a flannelboard. Give the birthday child the appropriate number of felt candles. Let him or her place the candles on the cake, one at a time, as the other children count.

101 Plastic Foam Cake

Stack three 1-inch thick plastic foam circles, one on top of another, and glue them together to make a "cake." Use colorful felt scraps to decorate the sides of the cake. Glue birthday candle holders to the top of the cake. On a child's birthday, put the appropriate number of candles in the

holders and then light the candles. Let the birthday child blow out the candles after everyone sings "Happy Birthday." (Caution: Adults should always supervise activities that involve lighted candles.)

102 Playdough Birthday Cake

Fill a cake pan with playdough. Set out candles, small plastic flowers and other decorative items. Let a child use the items to decorate the cake. Count the candles on the cake with the child. Ask him or her who the birthday cake is for, then sing "Happy Birthday" to that person.

103 Stars Chair Cover

Make the chair cover as described in prop 98. Cut star shapes out of felt or other fabric. Attach small strips of self-gripping fastener to the stars and to the chair cover. Let the birthday child put one star on the cover for each year old he or she is.

Blocks

104 **Cookie Sheets**
Give each child a cookie sheet. This gives the children flat surfaces on which to build and keeps small blocks in a more contained area.

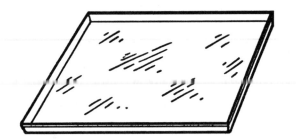

105 **Creative Play Props**
Add a variety of props to the block area to encourage creative play. Select props randomly or with a specific theme. Change the props regularly.

106 **Farm Props**
For a farm theme, set out toy fences, stuffed animals, plastic animals and straw hats in the block area.

107 **Fishing Props**
Collect fishing poles, life jackets, fishing nets and tackle boxes to put in the block area for a fishing theme.

108 **Floor Tiles**
Give the children large vinyl floor tiles on which to build.

109 **Maps**
Let the children build block cities and bridges on old road maps and city charts.

110 **Railroad Props**
Find an engineer hat, a whistle, tickets and suitcases to put in the block area for a train theme.

111 **Road Signs**
Set out small handmade road signs for the children to use when building roads, bridges and tunnels.

112 Travel Props

Set out suitcases, tickets, TV trays and aprons for use on a pretend airplane flight in the block area.

113 Zoo Props

Set out stuffed and plastic animals, a wagon, small brooms and zookeeper hats for block area zoo play.

Blocks to Make

114 Blocks From the Cupboard

Set out a collection of unopened food cans and boxes in various sizes and shapes. Let the children build with the cans and boxes.

115 Empty Food Box Blocks

Use empty food boxes, such as cookie and cereal boxes, to make blocks. Tape the tops closed and cover the boxes with bright self-stick paper.

116 Grocery Sack Blocks

Make large, lightweight blocks with grocery sacks. Stuff a sack with crumpled newspaper and tape the top down to create a rectangular block shape. Make as many blocks as desired.

117 Milk Carton Blocks

Cut the tops off half-gallon cardboard milk cartons and discard. Rinse and dry the cartons well. To make each block, you will need two cartons. Fill one of the cartons with crumpled newspaper for extra strength, if desired. Then slide the top of one carton over the top of the other. Tape the outside edges so that the cartons cannot be pulled apart. Make as many blocks as you wish.

118 Small Box Blocks

Use small boxes as inexpensive blocks. Stuff the boxes with crumpled newspaper, tape the lids shut and paint with favorite colors.

119 Wooden Blocks

Create blocks by sawing two-by-four wooden studs and large wooden dowels into a variety of lengths. Smooth out the rough edges of the blocks with sandpaper.

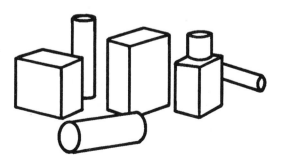

Communication Props

120 Bulletin Board

Make a large bulletin board out of corkboard, plasterboard or corrugated cardboard. Leave picture-type messages for the children on the board. Encourage the children to reply to your messages and leave messages for each other.

121 Cottage Cheese Container Phone

Poke small holes in the bottoms of two clean cottage cheese containers. Slip each container over a different end of a 6-foot piece of yarn. Tie knots at the ends of the yarn on the insides of the containers. Have one child hold one of the containers to his or her ear while another child talks into the other container. Be sure the children are holding the containers far enough apart to make the string taut between them.

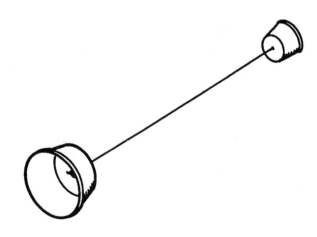

122 Fax Machine Fun

If you have access to a fax machine, bring it to your room for a day. Try to work with another group of children who have access to a fax machine. Let the children send messages and pictures back and forth.

123 Mailbox

Cover a shoebox with dark blue construction paper. Write "U.S. Mail" on both sides of the box. Let the children "mail" notes or pictures to each other. Once a day (or week) open the box and distribute the mail.

124 Message Boxes

Tape together several small boxes, tin cans or cardboard toilet tissue tubes. Label each box with a child's name. Encourage the children to leave messages, notes, artwork, etc., for each other.

125 Paper Cup Phone

Poke small holes in the bottoms of two paper cups. Tie a large knot on one end of a 6-foot piece of string or thick twine. Thread the string through one of the cups so that the long end hangs out of the bottom of the cup. Insert the long end of the string through the hole in the bottom of the other cup. Tie another knot on the end of the string. Make sure both knots are inside the cups. Let one child hold a cup up to his or her ear while another child talks into the other cup. Be sure the string is taut between the cups.

126 Survey Board

Divide a piece of white paper by drawing four horizontal lines two inches apart. Label the top of the paper something like "Pet Survey." Draw a picture at the beginning of each line to represent different kinds of pets. Attach the piece of paper to a clipboard and let the children survey classmates, friends, neighbors, etc. Have them place a check mark in the appropriate area when someone says they have a certain pet.

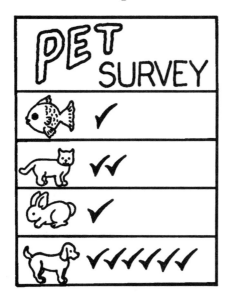

127 Survey Cards

Use a felt-tip marker to divide 5- by 7-inch index cards or posterboard pieces into four horizontal sections each. Cover the cards with clear self-stick paper. Use a crayon to label the top of each card with a topic like "Favorite Color Survey." Draw a picture at the beginning of each line to represent different colors. Attach the index card to a clipboard and let the children survey classmates, friends, neighbors, etc. Have them place a check mark in the appropriate area when someone says a certain color. Wipe the marks off the cards with a dry cloth when the children want to take another survey.

128 Telephone Booth

Draw a large rotary or push-button number pattern on the inside of a tall sturdy box. Using tape and string, attach a paper cup near the number pattern inside of the box.

129 Wall Phone

Cover a medium-sized shoebox with white paper. Draw a rotary dial in the appropriate place. Attach a string to the side of the box. Then attach a paper cup to the string for a receiver. Tape another paper cup under the dial for a mouthpiece.

Coordination Props

130 Balance Beam

Sand and stain a 6-foot long two-by-four to make a beam. Cut two 6-inch lengths and four 1-inch lengths from another two-by-four. Place two of the 1-inch lengths on top of a 6-inch length, lining up the outside edges. (See illustration.) This creates a 4-inch space for the beam to rest on. Nail the wood together. Repeat with the remaining 6-inch and 1-inch pieces. Place the beam in the holders.

131 Beanbag Balancing

Have the children practice walking around the room with beanbags balanced on their heads.

132 Beanbag Walking

Have the children balance beanbags on their arms and walk around in a circle.

133 Can And Clothespins

Set out a large coffee can or a cardboard ice cream container with some wooden slot-type clothespins. Let the children place the clothespins around the rim of the coffee can. Or have them stand over the can and drop the clothespins into it.

134 Cups And Saucers

Set out plastic cups and saucers. Let the children take turns stacking them. Have them see how many cups and saucers they can stack before the stack falls.

135 Masking Tape Path

Use masking tape to make a curving, double-lined path on the floor. Have the children walk down the path as fast as they can without stepping on the tape.

136 Yarn Walking

Lay a 6-foot piece of thick yarn on the floor. Let the children practice being baby elephants walking and balancing on the yarn piece.

Eye-Hand Coordination Props

137 Balloon

Blow up a balloon and tie the end. Have the children stand in a circle. Toss the balloon up and as it comes down have the child closest to it bat it up again. Let the children continue to bat the balloon without letting it touch the floor. If the group is large, try using two or three balloons.

138 Basic Beanbag

Fold a 5- by 8-inch piece of heavy fabric in half, right sides together. Stitch on two sides. Turn right side out and fill with small dried beans. Turn the open edges under and sew them closed.

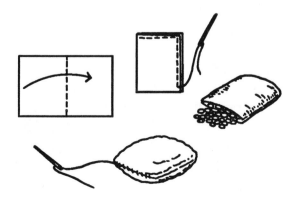

139 Beanbag Basket Targets

Let the children toss beanbags into laundry baskets, wicker baskets or other kinds of baskets.

140 Beanbag Hula-Hoop Targets

Let the children toss beanbags through Hula-Hoops.

141 Beanbag Yarn Circle Targets

Have the children toss bean bags into yarn circles on the floor.

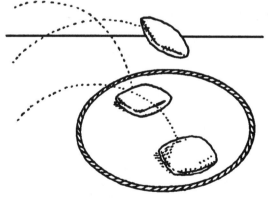

142 Blanket

Have the children hold up the edges of a blanket. Place a toy animal in the center of the blanket and let the children toss the animal up and down on the blanket.

143 Bracelet Rings

Let the children toss plastic bracelets over a ring toss peg.

144 Butterfly Catcher
Cut butterfly shapes out of lightweight paper. Throw them up into the air and let the children take turns catching them with a strainer.

145 Button Board
Cut off the front of an old shirt that has fairly large buttons and buttonholes. Button the shirt front and securely tape each side of it to a large piece of heavy cardboard. Let the children take turns buttoning and unbuttoning the shirt. (If the collar sags, stitch it in place on the cardboard.)

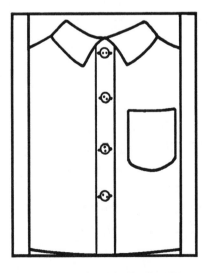

146 Cup Toss

Place a Ping-Pong ball in a large paper cup. Let the children take turns tossing the ball up out of the cup and catching it again.

147 Follow the Ball

Hang a plastic ball from the ceiling. Give a child a flashlight. Darken the room and swing the ball back and forth. Have the child follow the ball's movement with the flashlight beam.

148 Golf Box
Turn a large shoebox upside down and cut a hole in one side. Place some Ping-Pong balls on the floor. Let the children take turns using a yardstick to hit the balls into the hole in the shoebox.

149 Hammer And Nails

Set out nails with large heads, medium-sized hammers and small and large pieces of wood. Let the children hammer the nails into small individual pieces of wood or into one large piece. (Help them get started by hammering the nails far enough into the wood so that they stand up straight.)

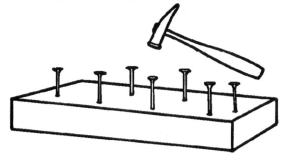

150 Indoor Balls

Crumple up two or three sheets of newspaper and stuff them into the toe of a nylon stocking. Tie a knot and cut off the rest of the stocking. Make as many as desired.

151 Indoor Racket

Stretch the bottom part of a coat hanger into a circular shape. Flatten the hook on the hanger by squeezing it toward the back of the stem and taping it to make a handle. Cover the circular part of the hanger with a piece of nylon stocking. Let the children take turns hitting a soft indoor ball with the racket.

152 Lacing Board

Cut out a 7- by 10-inch piece of sturdy cardboard and two 3- by 10-inch pieces of heavy vinyl. Place the vinyl pieces on top of the cardboard, leaving a 1-inch space down the middle. Use duct tape to attach the outside edges of the vinyl to the cardboard. Use a hole punch to punch holes down the inside edge of each vinyl piece. Then thread a long shoelace through the bottom holes. Let the children take turns lacing up the flaps.

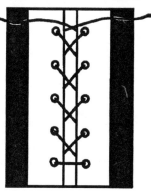

153 Newspaper Balls

Let the children toss pieces of crumpled newspaper back and forth with the scoop described in prop 164.

154 Nuts And Bolts

Set out a box full of large nuts and bolts. Have the children sort through them to find the ones that go together. Then let them screw the matching parts together.

155 Plants in a Row

Fill a shoebox with dirt and attach flower stickers to the tops of craft sticks. Have the children plant the stick flowers in the dirt in two or three straight rows. Encourage the children to plant their rows either from left to right or from back to front.

156 Plastic Foam Balls

Let the children play catch with plastic foam balls and the scoops described in prop 164.

157 Plastic Rings

Collect several small plastic container lids and cut out the center sections. Use these as rings for a ring toss game.

158 Plastic Straws

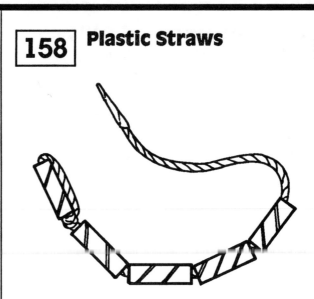

Set out plastic straws cut into 1-inch sections. For each child tie a 16-inch piece of yarn to one of the sections. Wrap the other end of the yarn with a piece of tape to make a "needle." Give each child one of the straw sections with yarn. Have the children string the remaining straw sections onto their yarn pieces.

159 Playdough Snakes

Have the children roll out long pieces of playdough or clay to make snakes. Show them how they can turn the playdough snakes into snails or baskets.

160 Ring Toss Holder

Put the lid on a large margarine container and turn the container upside down. Cut a hole the size of a cardboard paper towel tube in the middle of the container's base. Insert a cardboard paper towel tube in the hole. Set the container in the middle of the floor and let the children use it as a peg for a ring toss game.

161 Ring Toss Target
Turn a chair or stool upside down and let the children try to toss rings over the legs.

162 Rope Rings
Slip a wooden bead on a 12-inch piece of rope. Glue the ends of the rope together securely. Slide the bead over the glued ends and let dry. Follow the same procedure to make several rope rings.

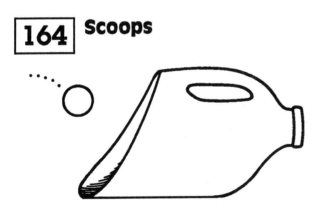

163 Rubber Gasket Rings
Have the children toss rubber canning jar gaskets over a ring toss peg.

164 Scoops

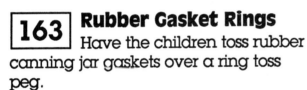

Clean and dry plastic bleach or detergent bottles that have handles. Use a craft knife to cut off the bottoms of the bottles at an angle. Smooth out any rough edges. Have the children toss Ping-Pong balls back and forth with the scoops.

165 Sock Balls
Stuff children's socks with two or three nylon stockings each and sew them closed.

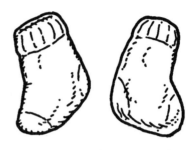

166 Sock Beanbag
Cut off the foot of an old cotton sock and fill it with small dried beans. Turn the open edges under and sew them together securely.

167 Screws And Screwdrivers
Set out large-headed screws, a medium-sized screwdriver and pieces of softwood. Let the children take turns screwing the screws into the wood.

168 Squirt Bottles

Set small empty paper cups on a ledge or piece of wood outdoors. Let the children take turns trying to knock over the cups by squirting water at them with squirt bottles.

169 Tire

Hang a tire from a tree. Be sure to hang it high enough so the children cannot swing on it. Set out easy-to-throw balls such as sponge-type balls, pompom balls and Ping-Pong balls. Have the children see how many balls they can throw through the tire.

170 Tongs

Let the children use a pair of tongs to transfer cotton balls, Ping-Pong balls, erasers or nuts from one container to another.

171 Tree Stump Hammering

Let the children take turns hammering nails into a large tree stump.

172 Tweezers

Let the children use a pair of tweezers to transfer dried beans, popcorn kernels, O-shaped cereal pieces or small straw sections from one container to another.

173 Wet Sponges

Let the children toss wet sponges back and forth outside.

174 Yarn Ball Catch Game

Wrap yarn around a 3-inch width of cardboard 25 times. Carefully slide the cardboard out and tie the yarn together in the middle with a 2-foot length of yarn. Clip the looped ends of the yarn and fluff them into a ball. Use the long piece of yarn to tie the yarn ball to the handle of the plastic bottle scoop described in prop 164. Let the children take turns tossing up and catching the yarn ball with the scoop.

175 Balls

Let the children use balls of all sizes and kinds to develop various coordination skills. Try to provide at least one ball per child. Balls can be used for throwing, bouncing, kicking and catching.

176 Blanket Toss

Set out a stuffed toy and a small blanket. Have two or four children hold the corners of the blanket and toss and catch the stuffed toy without letting it fall to the ground.

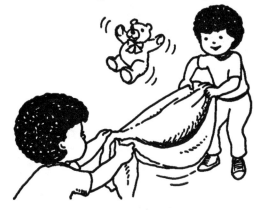

177 Broom Croquet

Give the children small brooms and balls. Place empty tin cans around the yard. Let the children use the brooms to move the balls from one can to the next. If desired, give the children a time limit and count how many cans they can hit in that amount of time.

178 Can Stilts

Collect two identical tin cans that hold a liquid, such as tomato sauce cans, small juice cans or chicken broth cans. Use a punch-type can opener to make a hole in the side of one can near the top. Make another hole opposite the first. Drain the liquid out of the can and save it to use at another time. Rinse out the can. Tape one end of a piece of rope to make a needle and thread the rope through the holes. Tie the rope so that the top of it reaches a child's waist when he or she stands on the can. Repeat for the second can. To use the can stilts, have a child stand with a foot on each can, hold onto the ropes and lift his or her hands and feet together to walk.

179 Flashlight Writing

Use masking tape to make a large shape, number or letter on a wall. Darken the room and let the children take turns tracing the shape with the beam of a flashlight.

180 Jack-Be-Nimble Candlestick

Place a candle in an unbreakable candle holder in the center of the floor. Have the children take turns jumping over the candle. Vary the height of the candle according to the abilities of the children. If desired, have the children recite the nursery rhyme "Jack Be Nimble" while they are jumping over the candlestick.

181 Kick Bag

Stuff an old pillowcase or a strong paper bag with crumpled newspaper. Sew or tape the end closed. Let the children take turns kicking the bag with their bare feet. Experiment with large and small pillowcases or bags to see which ones work best in your space.

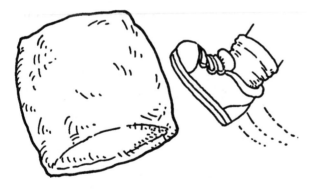

182 Ladder Walk

Place an extension ladder flat on the floor. Let the children take turns stepping between the rungs. To increase the difficulty, raise the ladder a few inches off the ground by setting it on wooden blocks.

183 Newspaper Sticks

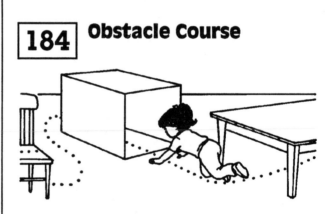

Lay two sheets of newspaper out flat, one on top of the other. Starting in one corner, roll the papers up into one long stick. Tape the loose corner in the middle of the stick. Make several sticks and let them use these sticks to jump over, throw through a tire or hold over their heads and behind their backs.

184 Obstacle Course

Set up an obstacle course for the children, using tables, chairs, tunnels and other large objects. Let the children take turns crawling under, climbing over, crawling through and going around the objects.

185 Pillows

Place small pillows on the floor and have the children practice hopping over them. If desired, have them pretend to be grasshoppers hopping about in a field.

186 River Rocks

Make rocks or stepping stones out of large pieces of cardboard or carpet squares. Have the children pretend that most of the floor is a river too wide to jump across. Have them leap from one rock to another to get across the river without falling in the water.

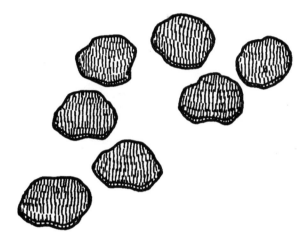

187 Rope Walk

Lay a rope on the floor in a circle or in a long line. Let the children pretend to be tightrope walkers and walk on the rope. Have them pretend that they are carrying an umbrella for balance. Tell them to be careful not to lose their balance.

188 Slithering Snake

Place a 10-foot length of rope on the floor. Have two children move the ends back and forth to make the rope look like a wiggling snake. Ask the rest of the children to pretend that the harmless snake has come out to play in the warm sunshine. Then let them take turns jumping over the snake while it is moving, trying not to startle it by stepping on its back.

189 Sponge Fun

Let the children use sponges to help wash windows or tables. Encourage them to move their arms up and down and back and forth.

190 Yarn River

Use two long pieces of string or yarn to mark off a section of floor to represent a river. Let the children practice jumping across the river. Make the river wider and wider as the children become stronger in their jumping.

Counting Props

191 Beads

Place large wooden beads on a table and let the children count them. String them on a shoelace or a piece of yarn. Let the children slide the beads back and forth as they count them. Or place them on a wooden dowel. Let the children count the beads as they slide them off the dowel.

192 Blocks

Let the children play with brightly colored blocks. Have them count the blocks as they stack them and build with them. Let the children stack the blocks according to color, shape or size and count them.

193 Bread Bag Fasteners

Gather together several colors and sizes of plastic bread bag fasteners. Give them to the children in a cup or an envelope. Let the children count all of the fasteners. Or have them sort the fasteners according to color or size then count them.

194 Cardboard Shapes

Using different colors of lightweight cardboard (gift boxes work well), cut out simple shapes. Have the children count all the red shapes, all of the grey shapes, all of the brown shapes, etc. Then have them count all of the squares, all of the circles, all of the triangles, etc.

195 Clothespins

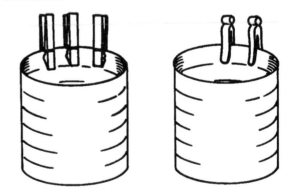

Collect spring-type and slot-type clothespins. Give them to the children in two empty coffee cans. Have the children sort the clothespins and count how many of each kind there are. Then have them place all of the spring-type clothespins around the rim of one coffee can and all of the slot-type clothespins around the rim of the other coffee can.

196 Crayons

Give the children a large box of crayons. Let them dump the crayons out of the box and sort them by color. Then have them count each group of crayons.

197 Dominoes

Let the children use a set of dominoes as counters. Have them turn the dominoes dotted-sides down. Let them count the dominoes as they line them up end to end or place them side by side.

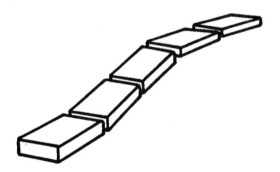

198 Felt Shapes

Cut small seasonal shapes out of 1-inch-square felt pieces. Let the children count the shapes on a table or a flannelboard.

199 Leaves

During the fall, take the children outside and let them gather various types of leaves. Have them sort the leaves by type. Then let the children count the leaves. Make a graph of the types of leaves and the number of leaves in each group.

200 Plastic Figures

Gather together a variety of small plastic toys, such as cars, animals, people, trees and blocks, and put them in a bucket. Label the bucket "1-2-3 Toys." Let the children take turns dumping out the contents of the bucket, sorting the toys by color or type and counting them.

201 Poker Chips

Give the children a box containing red, white and blue poker chips. Let them sort the chips by color and then count them.

202 Rocks

Collect several small, smooth rocks and place them in a basket. Give them to the children and let them count the rocks as they play and build things with them.

203 Seeds

Cut pumpkin or watermelon shapes out of construction paper. Give each child a reclosable plastic bag with some pumpkin or watermelon seeds in it. Have the children glue a certain number of seeds onto their shapes.

204 Shells

Collect several types of small shells. Place the shells in a large bucket or pan of water. Let the children reach into the bucket and "fish" for a handful of shells. Have the children count the number of shells they "catch."

205 Sponge Shapes

Cut counters out of sponges. Square, circle, triangle and rectangle shapes make good counting tools for children.

206 Spools

Gather together empty spools. String them on a shoelace and let the children slide them back and forth as they count them. Or let the children count the spools as they slide them onto a dowel.

207 Stepping Stones

Cut twenty large stone shapes out of construction paper, posterboard, cardboard or pieces of vinyl. Number the stone shapes 1 through 20. Place them on the floor and let the children count them as they step or leap from one to the other.

208 Stickers

Place different numbers of stickers on cardboard squares or large circular pricing tags with metal edges (available at office supply stores). Let the children count the number of stickers on each pricing tag or piece of cardboard.

209 Toothpicks

Give the children a small handful of different colored, dull-ended toothpicks. Count all the toothpicks with the group or have the children count them by color. Or bundle the toothpicks in groups of ten with a rubber band. Use the bundles to teach the numbers 10, 20, 30, etc. Be sure to supervise the children at all times when they are using toothpicks.

210 Wooden Cutouts

Collect thin wooden cutouts (available from many craft stores). Either leave them the natural wood color or paint them with bright enamel paint. Let the children use the wooden shapes as counters.

211 Yarn

Cut several different colors and types of yarn into 3-inch pieces. Place all the pieces in a box. Let the children place the pieces on a flannelboard, rug or table as they count them. Or have the children sort the yarn pieces into piles by color and then count the number of yarn pieces in each pile.

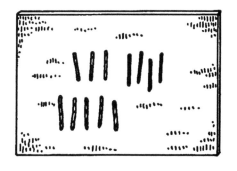

Creative
Movement Props

212 Ankle Bells

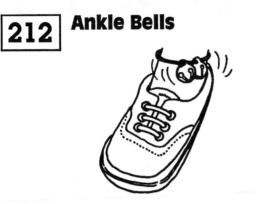

String one or two jingle bells on a piece of elastic and tie the ends together. Make one for each child. Let the children put on the ankle bells and wear them while they are dancing or prancing around.

213 Balloon

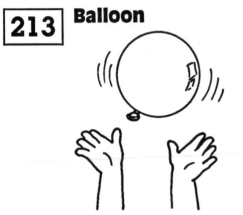

Blow up a balloon. Toss it in the air and let one of the children try to keep it from touching the ground. When the balloon touches the ground, another child gets a turn.

214 Balls

Set out a basket of various sizes and kinds of balls. Let the children experiment by bouncing and rolling all of the balls. Have the children observe how the balls bounce and roll. Later put the balls away and have the children pretend to be balls and roll and bounce around the room.

215 Cardboard Tubes

Save cardboard paper towel and gift wrap tubes. Give a tube to each child. Encourage the children to think of ways to use the tubes. For example, the tubes can become fishing poles, telescopes, rowing oars, batons, paintbrushes or stirring spoons.

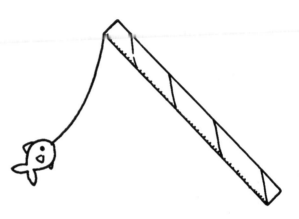

216 Drum

Beat out rhythms on a drum. Have the children walk slowly when you beat a slow rhythm, then faster and faster as you increase the tempo.

217 Elastic Loops

For each child cut a 3-foot section of ½-inch elastic and sew the ends together. Give each child a loop of elastic. Have the children stand on their loops and pull them up as high as possible; stretch the elastic as far out as possible with their arms; and loop the elastic around one of their feet, stretch it up high with one of their hands and swing their feet back and forth. Then let children experiment with other ways to use their loops.

218 Fabric Strips

Cut fabric into long wide strips. Have the children stand in two lines facing each other. Give each pair of facing children one of the strips. Have the children hold the ends of the strips and move them up and down to create waves. If desired, play a tape of ocean sounds while they are moving their fabric strips.

219 Feather

Have the children watch as you toss a feather up in the air and let it float slowly to the ground. Then let them pretend to be feathers and slowly float to the ground.

220 Fish Net

Have the children form a circle and hold onto the outer edges of a lightweight fish net. Have them toss up the net and try to get under it before it comes down.

221 Mattress

Locate an old clean mattress. Let the children use it for tumbling, jumping and rolling. Or place it under an indoor climbing toy to soften falls.

222 Pompoms

Cut 2-foot lengths out of two colors of crepe paper. Hold five pieces of each color together and tape them in the middle. Crinkle up the ends of the crepe paper. Make one or two pompoms for each child.

223 Rhythm Sticks

Use rhythm sticks to tap out rhythms for the children to move to.

224 Ribbon Wands

Roll up a piece of construction paper from corner to corner and tape it in place to make a stick wand. Attach a 5-foot piece of ribbon or crepe paper to the stick wand. Make as many as desired. Have the children whirl and twirl the wands around as they dance to gentle music.

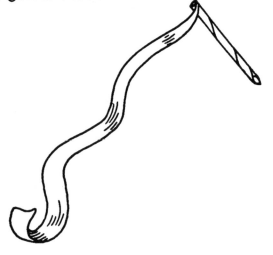

225 Scarves

Set out a box of sheer scarves and let each child choose one. Have the children pretend that their scarves are wings, sails or capes.

226 Small Towels

Give each child a towel. Have the children place their towels on a smooth floor and sit on them. Show the children how to hold onto the edges of their towels and use them to scoot or spin around on the floor.

227 Streamers

Cut 2-foot lengths of crepe paper, ribbon, plastic bag strips, newspaper strips or plastic surveyor's tape (available at hardware stores). Put ten of the strips together and staple them at one end to make a streamer. Make one for each child.

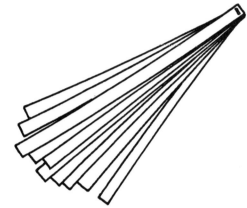

228 Streamers On Rings

Tape 2-foot crepe paper or ribbon streamers to large wooden or plastic rings. Plastic rings can be made by cutting the centers out of plastic lids. Have each child hold onto one or two of the rings and dance around the room.

229 Tube Streamers

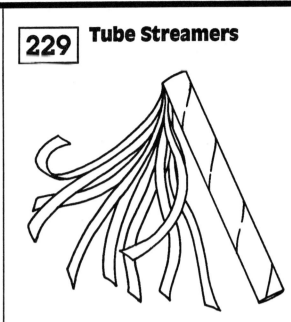

Attach streamers to the ends of cardboard paper towel tubes. Have each child tap two of them together for rhythm sticks or wave them around during movement time. Tube streamers also make great marching batons.

230 Waxed Paper Strips

Tear off long pieces of waxed paper. Have the children stand in two lines facing each other. Give each pair of facing children one of the long pieces. Have the children hold the ends of the waxed paper and move them up and down to create waves.

231 Yarn

Give each child a 4-foot piece of yarn. Have the children place their yarn pieces in straight lines on the floor. Then give them directions such as these: "Walk forward on the yarn. Walk backward. Hop over the yarn. Jump over the yarn." Then let them jump in and out of circles they make with their yarn pieces.

Dress-Up Props

Capes

Basic Cape

232 Start with a 2- by 2½-foot piece of fabric. Hem all of the edges, if desired. Fold over 1 inch of fabric on one of the 2-foot sides of the material and stitch to make a casing for elastic. Thread 14 inches of elastic through the casing. Sew the ends of the elastic together, leaving enough room for a child to slide the cape over his or her head.

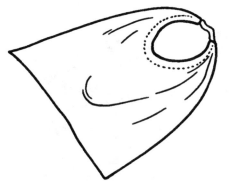

Crepe Paper Cape

233 Tape colored crepe paper strips to a long piece of yarn. Safety-pin the center of the yarn piece to the back of a child's collar and tie the yarn ends together in front.

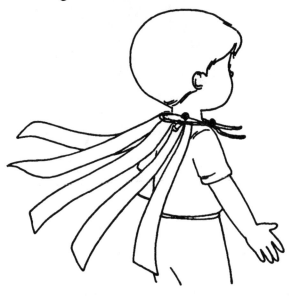

234 Tea Towel Cape

Use scissors to snip small holes, about 2 inches apart, across one of the ends of an old, lightweight tea towel. Thread a piece of yarn through the holes. Tie large enough knots near the ends of the yarn so they will not slide out of the holes.

Ears

235 Antennae

Cover a plastic headband with foil. Attach foil balls to it with pipe cleaners to make antennae.

236 Bear Ears

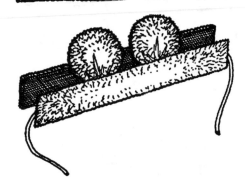

Cut two 2- by 12-inch rectangles and two 4-inch bear ear shapes out of fuzzy brown material. Gather the ear shapes slightly at the bottom. Sew the long edges of the two rectangles together with the ear shapes in between so that the ears stand up. (See illustration.) Attach ribbons to the sides of the rectangles for ties. Use different-sized ear shapes and various colors and textures of fabric for other animal ears.

237 Headband Ears

Cut two ear shapes out of fabric, felt or posterboard. Tape or glue the ears to a plastic headband. (Plastic headbands are available at drugstores.)

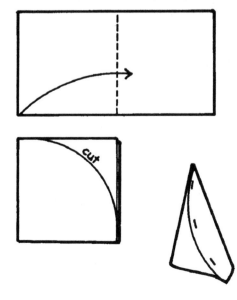

Hats

238 Basic Cone Hat

Fold a piece of large construction paper in half and cut out a quarter circle. Unfold the paper to make a half-circle. Roll the half-circle into a cone shape and staple or tape it together. Decorate it as desired.

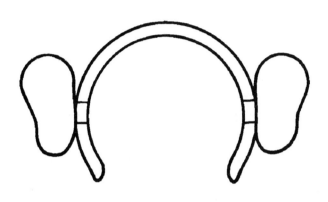

239 Clown Hat

Cut a large circle out of construction paper. Cut the circle halfway through and roll it into a cone shape to fit a child's head. Tape the edges in place. Decorate the hat with pompoms and felt-tip marker designs. Attach yarn to the sides of the hat for ties.

240 Hat Box

Gather several types of hats and keep them in a box in the dress-up area. Thrift stores are a good place to find inexpensive hats. Possible hats for your box are baseball caps, bathing caps, crowns, firefighter hats, fishing caps, hard hats, rain hats, straw hats, stocking caps, sun bonnets, top hats and western hats.

241 Mini Hat

Turn a medium-sized paper cup upside down and decorate it as desired with stickers, yarn, felt-tip marker designs, etc. Glue a cotton ball on top of the cup. Attach yarn to the sides of the cup for ties.

242 Newspaper Hat

Fold a 24- by 28-inch piece of newsprint in half crosswise. Fold it in half again. With the second fold at the top, fold over the two sides of the paper so that they meet in the middle, forming a triangle. Fold up the bottom edges of the paper twice to make a hat rim and secure the edges with tape. Decorate the hat with brightly colored stickers.

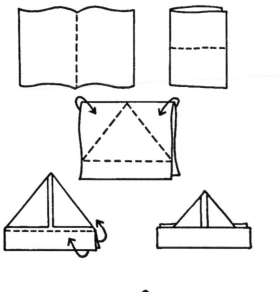

243 Paper Bag Wig

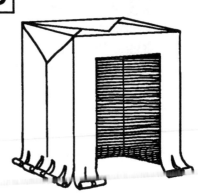

Cut a large rectangle from the front section of a large brown paper grocery bag, leaving about two inches on the sides and bottom of the bag. Turn the bag upside down and cut a fringe around the bottom. Curl the fringe by tightly rolling each section around a pencil and holding it there for about 30 seconds.

244 Parade Hat

Make one cut from the rim to the center of a paper plate. Overlap the two cut edges and tape or staple them together. Attach yarn to the sides of the hat to use for tying under a child's chin. Decorate the hat as desired with flowers, stickers or crepe paper streamers.

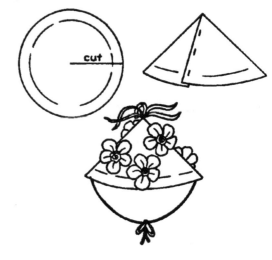

245 Top Hat

Tape a piece of construction paper around an oatmeal box or other round cardboard container. Turn the box so that the opening is at the bottom. Glue a construction paper brim to the bottom edge. Decorate the top part of the hat as desired. Attach yarn to the sides of the hat for ties.

246 Twirling Cap

Make a cone-shaped hat out of construction paper and cut off the top to make a small hole. Tape crepe paper strips around the inside of the hat (near the top) and pull them out through the hole. Attach yarn to the sides of the hat for ties.

247 Wallpaper Hat

To make a hat, you will need two 20-inch squares of wallpaper. Spread glue over the back of one of the wallpaper squares. Then place the second square on top of the first, backs together. Press the squares together from the center out, to squeeze out any excess glue. Place the double square over a child's head and mold it into a fancy hat. Tie a string around the band of the hat to help it keep its shape. Remove the hat from the child's head and let it dry. When the hat is dry, remove the string and cut the brim into the desired shape. Decorate the hat as desired with flowers, ribbons, fabric scraps, lace or bows.

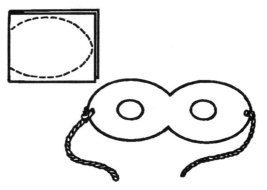

Masks

248 Basic Eye Mask

Fold a 3- by 8-inch piece of construction paper in half. Starting at the fold, draw one half of an eye mask shape. Cut the shape out of the paper. Unfold the paper to make a whole mask. Cut out eye holes. Attach yarn to the sides of the mask to use for tying behind a child's head.

249 | Diver's Mask

Cut a 2½-inch section out of an oatmeal box or other round cardboard container that measures 4 inches across. Cut a notch to fit over a child's nose in one end of the cardboard section. Place a piece of clear plastic wrap over the other end and secure it with a rubber band. Cover the outside of the cardboard section with construction paper. Attach thick yarn to the sides of the mask to use for tying behind the child's head.

250 | Egg Carton Mask

Cut two adjoining cup sections out of an egg carton. Cut a hole in the bottom of each section. Attach a piece of elastic string to the sides of the mask to hold it in place around a child's head.

251 | Flower Mask

Cut the center out of a paper plate. Turn the plate over and glue construction paper petals around the rim (or cut notches around the outside of the rim to make petals and paint the entire rim in a bright color). Attach yarn to the sides of the mask to use for tying behind a child's head.

252 | Forehead Mask

To make a mask that won't interfere with a child's seeing or breathing, cut the desired mask face shape out of construction paper and attach it to a paper headband that fits around a child's forehead. Make sure that the bottom of the mask face is above the child's eyes.

253 | Leopard Mask

Cut eye holes out of a paper plate. Paint the backside of the plate yellow. When the paint has dried, use a black felt-tip marker or black paint to make spots. Glue on nose and ear shapes and add tissue paper strips around the edge of the plate. Attach a tongue depressor handle for a child to hold the mask in front of his or her face.

254 | Zebra Mask

Cut eye holes out of a paper plate. Leave the paper plate white and paint the back side of the plate with vertical black stripes. Glue on nose and ear shapes and add tissue paper strips around the edge of the plate. Attach a tongue depressor handle for a child to hold the mask in front of his or her face.

Noses

255 | Master Disguise

Cut two adjoining rings out of a plastic six-pack holder to make a pair of glasses. Wrap pipe cleaners around each side of the glasses and bend them to fit around a child's ears. Attach an egg carton cup to the bottom of the glasses to make a nose. Attach a mustache made out of cotton or felt to the bottom of the nose.

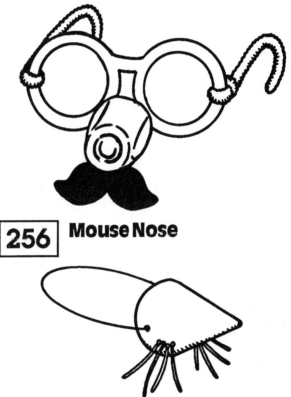

256 | Mouse Nose

Cut a small circle out of black construction paper. Cut the circle halfway through, roll it into a cone shape and tape the edges in place. For whiskers, thread thin pieces of black yarn through the nose shape (from the inside to the outside) knotting each whisker on the inside and the outside to hold it in place. Attach a loop of elastic thread to the sides of the nose to hold it in place.

Shoes

257 Felt Feet
Cut two foot shapes (or paw shapes) out of felt. Cut two holes in the top of each shape. Place the felt feet on top of a child's laced shoes. Thread the shoelaces through the holes in the felt feet and tie them.

258 Monster Shoes
Put the lids on two shoeboxes and tape them securely closed. Cut a hole in the lid of each box that is just large enough for a child's foot to fit in. Use crayons or felt-tip markers to decorate the boxes, if desired.

259 Shoe Box
Collect several different pairs of old shoes from thrift stores. Place them in a large box in the dress-up area. Let the children use the shoes to add to imaginary and dramatic play. Suggestions for types of shoes to put in the box are tennis shoes, sandals, slippers, hiking boots, snow boots and high heels.

Wings

260 Bird Wings
Tape colored crepe paper strips to a long piece of yarn. Safety-pin the center of the yarn to the back of a child's collar and tie the ends of the yarn around the child's wrists.

261 Butterfly Wings
Use two colorful scarves (or squares of filmy material) to make butterfly wings. Safety-pin the scarves to the sleeves of a child's long-sleeved shirt.

More Dress-Up Props

262 Box Animal
Cut the top and the bottom out of a large cardboard box. On opposite sides of the box, cut oblong holes near the top edges for handles. Decorate the four sides of the box to make it look like an animal. Have a child step inside the box and hold it up by the handles as he or she walks around.

263 Clown Collar

Cut a large donut shape out of white felt or other fabric. Make the hole in the middle large enough for a child to slip his or her head through. Decorate the clown collar as desired with felt scraps.

264 Color Glasses

Cut two adjoining egg cups from an egg carton and cut the bottoms out of the egg cups. Cover the bottom of each egg cup with a different color of cellophane. Attach elastic string to the sides of the egg cups to keep the glasses in place on a child's face.

265 Crepe Paper Skirt

Tape strips of crepe paper to a long piece of ribbon or yarn. Leave the ends of the ribbon free to use as ties. Tie the skirt around a child's waist.

266 Newspaper Costumes

Let the children use newspaper to create silly costumes. They could make hats, stuff rolled-up papers into their clothes, tear paper to make neck holes or armholes or fringe the paper. The use of tape is optional. Newspaper ink can smear, so have the children wear old play clothes.

267 Scarves

Collect a variety of scarves. Thrift shops are a good source. Two or three tucked around a belt or in a waistband can become a beautiful dancing skirt. One tied around the shoulders can become a cape. One tied around a head can become a pirate hat. Scarves tied onto arms can become wings.

268 Star Wand

Cut a star shape out of cardboard and cover it with aluminum foil. Spread some glue on the front of the foil-covered star and sprinkle on glitter. After the glue dries, attach a dowel to the back of the star with glue or tape.

Holiday Props

269 | Advent Calendar

Save a ready-made Advent calendar from the previous year. Carefully remove the backing from the calendar. Place a white piece of paper over the backing and lightly trace around each square. Draw a picture or write a few words in each square on the paper. Put the new backing and the old front together and tape or glue them in place. Then use your new personalized Advent calendar in the usual way.

270 | Advent Wreath

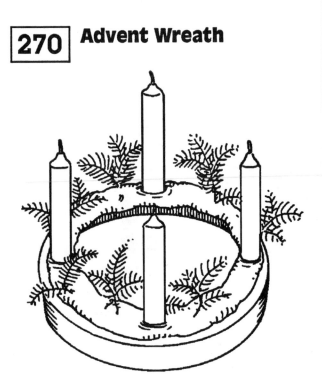

Cut a hole out of the center of a plastic lid. Roll a lump of playdough into a "snake" and press it into the lid. Stand four purple or red candles in the playdough. Decorate the top of the wreath with evergreen sprigs. (Note: The candles in the Advent wreath are not meant to be lighted.)

271 | Bell

Cut out an egg cup from a cardboard egg carton. Paint the inside and outside of the egg cup then dip the edges of the egg cup in glitter. Poke a pipe cleaner through the center of the cup. Make a hook out of the top half of the pipe cleaner and roll the bottom half up inside the cup to make a bell clapper.

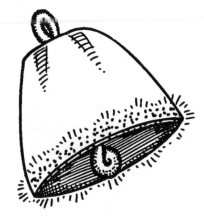

272 | Christmas Calendar

Cut a large Christmas tree shape out of green butcher paper or construction paper. Hang the tree shape on a wall or a bulletin board. Make a chain out of 24 strips of red construction paper. Arrange the chain on the tree. Starting on December 1, have a child remove one of the loops on the chain each day. When the last loop is removed, it will be Christmas Eve.

273 Christmas Tree

Set up a small artificial Christmas tree in a corner of the room. Let the children decorate the tree with handmade ornaments or ornaments you have provided. Use the tree as a teaching tool by giving the children directions such as these: "Put all the green ornaments on the tree; Take off all the red ornaments; Put a stocking ornament next to a reindeer ornament."

274 Elf Hat

Cut a large triangle out of a piece of red or green fabric. Fold the triangle in half, right sides together. Machine- or hand-stitch the open edges opposite the fold together. Then turn the triangle right side out. Add such details as a pompom top or fur brim as desired.

275 Fabric Stocking

Cut two stocking shapes out of felt. Place the shapes on top of each other and machine- or hand-stitch around the sides, leaving the top open. Cut simple Christmas shapes out of contrasting colors of felt and glue them on the front of the stocking. Add a ribbon loop to the top of the stocking for hanging.

276 Fireplace

Set out a large cardboard appliance box. Cut a fireplace opening out of one side of the box. Use paints, felt-tip markers or crayons to decorate the box to look like a fireplace.

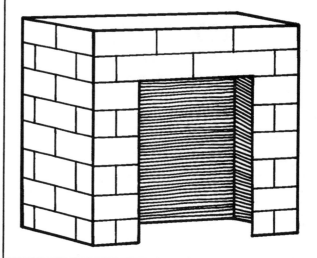

277 Grocery Bag Stocking

Pull a large brown grocery bag apart at the seams and fold it inside out. Then cut a large stocking shape out of the bag, with the fold forming the back on the stocking. Use a hole punch to punch holes around the open side and bottom edges of the shape. Lace the stocking shape closed with red or green yarn. Decorate as desired.

278 Hand Shape Antlers

Trace around a child's hands on a piece of construction paper and cut out the shapes. Cut a 2-inch-wide headband out of construction paper. Tape the hand shapes to the headband. Adjust the headband to fit around the child's head and tape the ends together.

279 Logs

Roll up large brown grocery bags and fasten the ends in place with masking tape or rubber bands to make logs.

280 Reindeer Antlers

Collect two small twigs. Cut a 2-inch-wide headband out of construction paper. Tape the twigs to the headband. Adjust the headband to fit around a child's head and tape the ends together.

Easter Props

281 Bunny Basket

Cut a half-gallon cardboard milk carton down to the last 6 inches. Brush glue on the sides of the carton and cover them completely with triple-sized cotton balls. Make a bunny face on the front of the carton with construction paper eyes, a cotton ball nose and pipe cleaner whiskers. Glue white construction paper ear shapes to the top front edge of the bunny basket. Then glue an additional cotton ball to the back of the basket for a bunny tail. Add a handle and some Easter grass to complete.

282 Bunny Ears Hat

Make a bunny ears hat out of a large piece of white construction paper. Cut two bunny ear shapes in the construction paper as shown. Fold the center of the paper down. Fold over the right side of the paper and staple it to the middle section. Repeat with the left side. Turn the hat over and color the center of the ears pink. Fold the ears down, if desired. Staple yarn on both sides of the hat for ties.

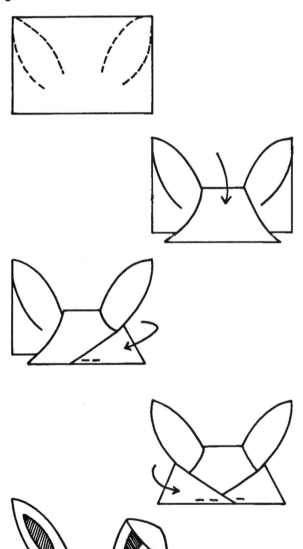

283 Easter Calendar

Cut a large basket shape out of construction paper. Hang the basket shape on a wall. Cut out one construction paper egg shape for each day left before Easter. Arrange the egg shapes in and around the basket shape. Each day, have a child remove one of the egg shapes. When all the eggs are gone, it will be Easter.

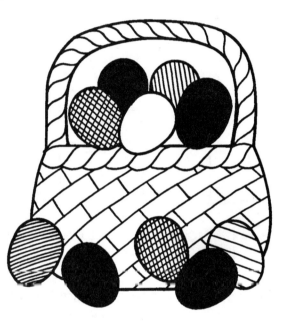

284 Easter Egg Tree

Paint a tree branch with tempera paint. Stand the branch in a pot of sand. Hang blown eggs that have been dyed, paper egg shapes or plastic eggs from the branches. Add ribbon bows, if desired.

285 Egg Stands

Cut cardboard toilet tissue tubes into 1- to 2-inch sections to make egg stands. Decorate the egg stands with self-stick paper, stickers, crayons or felt-tip markers.

286 | Paper Bag Bunny Basket

Cut off the top half of three sides of a white paper bag, leaving the front of the bag whole. Cut ear shapes out of the top half of the front of the bag as shown. Make a bunny face on the front of the bag with felt-tip markers or crayons and add a cotton ball tail to the back.

287 | Wicker Basket Calendar

Set out a real wicker basket. Fill the basket with one plastic egg for each day left before Easter. Each day, have a child remove one egg. When all the eggs are gone, it will be Easter.

Halloween Props

288 | Face Paint

In a small bowl, combine 5 teaspoons cornstarch, 1 teaspoon white flour and 2 teaspoons shortening. Add 1½ teaspoons glycerine (available at drug stores) and mix thoroughly. Use food coloring to dye the face paint the colors you want. Carefully apply the paint to a child's face. The make-up removes easily with cold cream or baby oil.

289 | Glowing Jack-O'-Lantern

Turn a paper lunch sack upside down and cut a jack-o'-lantern face out of the front of it. Open up the sack and put it over a small flashlight. Gather the bottom of the sack around the flashlight and fasten it in place with a rubber band. Turn on the flashlight to make the jack-o'-lantern glow.

290 | Halloween Calendar Scene

Just before the beginning of October, create a Halloween bulletin board scene that includes a large, bare tree. Cut 31 leaf shapes out of construction paper. Attach the leaves to the bulletin board tree with tacks or pins. Each day have a leaf "fall" from a branch to the ground under the tree. Then count with the children the number of leaves left on the branches. The day that the last leaf falls will be Halloween.

291 Scarecrow

Stuff a small paper bag with newspaper. Close the bag with a twist tie or a piece of yarn. Turn the bag upside down and draw a scarecrow face on the front of it. Tape the bag to the top of a coat hanger. Put an old shirt or coat on the hanger and add a hat to the top of the bag. Then hang up the scarecrow in the room.

292 Sleeper Costume

Start with an old blanket sleeper in a size the children can wear. Dye the sleeper and add details with fabric, pompoms, yarn and ribbon. For example, you could make a mouse costume by dyeing the sleeper gray and adding felt ears and yarn whiskers. Or you could dye a sleeper yellow or orange and add a fabric collar and pompom buttons to make a clown costume.

293 Trick-Or-Treat Box

Remove the lid from an oatmeal box or other cylindrical container. Cover the box with plain self-stick paper and decorate with stickers. Punch two holes opposite each other near the top of the box. Thread a piece of yarn or ribbon through the holes to make a handle.

294 Trick-Or-Treat Jug

Cut the top off of a plastic gallon milk jug, leaving the handle intact. Glue on construction paper eye, nose, mouth and ear shapes to make a "monster face." Then glue pieces of yarn around the top edge of the jug for hair.

Cardboard Tube Candles
Paint cardboard toilet tissue tubes with tempera paint. When the tubes are dry, glue them upright on small paper plates. Add a red, orange or yellow construction paper flame shape to the top of each candle.

296 | Chain Calendar

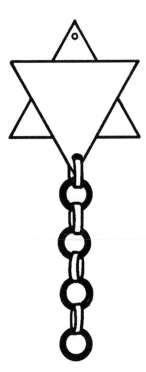

Cut two large identical triangles out of yellow construction paper. Make a Star of David by placing one triangle point up and gluing the second triangle point down on top of it. Make a chain out of four strips of blue construction paper and four strips of white construction paper. Attach the chain to the Star of David. Hang up the calendar and let a child remove one of the loops for each day of Hanukkah.

297 | Cotton Swab Dreidle
Cut a 2-inch square out of heavy paper. Using a ruler as a guide, draw two diagonal lines across the square from corner to corner and write the Hebrew letters "nun," "gimel," "hay" and "shin" in the four sections. (See illustration.) Use a large needle to poke a hole in the center of the square where the lines intersect. Remove the cotton from one end of a cotton swab and insert the swab halfway through the hole, cotton end down. Adjust the square so that it is perpendicular to the swab and squeeze drops of glue around the hole to hold the square in place. Allow the glue to dry before using the dreidle.

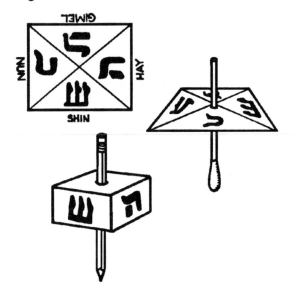

298 | Milk Carton Dreidle
Fold down the top of a ½-pint cardboard milk carton and tape it in place. Cover the carton with self-stick paper. Use a permanent felt-tip marker to write the Hebrew letters "nun," "gimel," "hay" and "shin" on the four sides. (See illustration.) Poke a chopstick or a pencil through the box and secure it with tape.

299 Playdough Menorah

Cut a 1- by 8-inch strip from cardboard. Cover the cardboard strip with playdough. Put a large birthday candle in the middle of the playdough to use for a shammash ("server candle"). Then put four small birthday candles on each side of the shammash. (Note: The candles in the menorah are not meant to be lighted.)

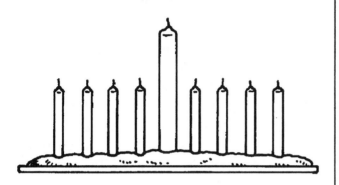

300 Spool Menorah

Collect eight small empty spools and one large empty spool. Glue the spools to a 2- by 12-inch piece of wood with the large spool in the middle and four small spools on each side of it. Put birthday candles in the holes in the tops of the spools. (Note: The candles in the menorah are not meant to be lighted.)

301 Star Of David

Glue three craft sticks together in a triangle. Make two triangles. Glue the triangles together with one triangle point up and one triangle point down. Decorate as desired.

St. Patrick's Day Props

302 Cast Iron Pot-Of-Gold

Use a cast iron kettle as a pot-of-gold. Fill it with "gold coins" or "gold nuggets."

303 Gold Coins

Cut small circles out of cardboard. Cover each circle with a piece of gold foil to make a gold coin.

304 Gold Nuggets

Collect several small rocks in a variety of shapes. Spray-paint the rocks gold to use as gold nuggets.

305 Ice Cream Bucket Pot-Of-Gold

Find a cardboard ice cream bucket and spray-paint it black to make a pot-of-gold. Fill it with gold coins or nuggets.

Thanksgiving Props

306 Indian Necklace

Smooth a brown or white coffee filter out flat. Make a cut through the ribbed edge of the filter, then cut out the center. Punch a hole in each end of the filter and attach 10-inch pieces of yarn for ties. Decorate the filter with felt-tip markers. Then cut a fringe along the outer edge to complete.

307 Indian Vest

Cut a neck hole in the bottom of a large brown paper bag and two armholes in the sides. Cut open the front of the bag from the bottom edge up to the neck hole. Use crayons to decorate the bag with Indian symbols or other designs. Cut a fringe along the bottom edge of the vest.

308 Pilgrim Bonnet

Cut and discard the top half of a small white paper bag. Roll the top of the bag over to make a cuff. Then carefully cut off one of the wide sides of the bag. Punch a hole in each narrow side and attach pieces of yarn or ribbon for ties.

309 Pilgrim Collar

Cut a neck hole out of the middle of a piece of white construction paper. Then make a cut up to the neck hole in the middle of one of the long sides of the paper.

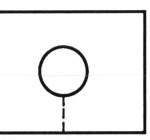

310 Pilgrim Hat

Cut three-fourths of a circle out of the middle of a circular piece of black construction paper. (See illustration.) Fold up the partial circle and cut it into a square shape. Then glue a yellow construction paper buckle shape to the square.

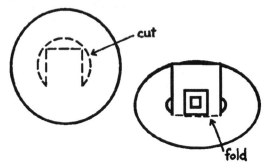

Valentine's Day Props

311 | Heart Box Puzzle

Trace around a heart-shaped candy box on a piece of red or pink construction paper or posterboard. Cut out the heart shape, then cut it into puzzle pieces. Let the children take turns using the box as a puzzle holder while putting the pieces of the heart together.

312 | Heart Cake

Use your favorite recipe to prepare cake batter. Pour the batter into one round pan and one square pan. Bake according to the recipe directions. Make a platter for the cake by covering a large piece of cardboard with foil. Place the square cake on the platter with one corner facing downward. Then cut the round cake in half and place the halves against the top two sides of the square cake to make a heart shape. Cover the entire cake with frosting and decorate as desired.

313 | Heart Stamp

Cut a heart shape out of a plastic foam food tray. Cut a 1- by 4-inch strip out of cardboard. Fold the strip in half, fold up the ends, then tape the ends to the back of the plastic foam heart to make a handle.

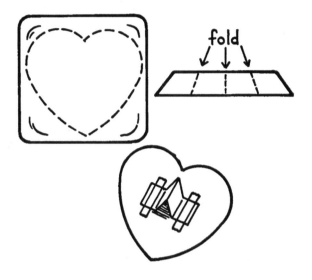

314 | Valentine Mailbox

Place a white paper lunch bag flat on a table. Glue red and blue strips cut from construction paper across the top and bottom of the bag. At the top of the back side of the bag, use a brass paper fastener to attach a small flag shape cut from red construction paper.

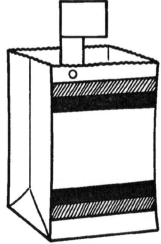

315 Arbor Day Trees

Collect two cardboard toilet tissue tubes and one paper plate. Cut two slits directly opposite each other in one end of each toilet tissue tube. Cut the paper plate in half. Paint the tubes brown to make trunks. Then use crayons or felt-tip markers to decorate the paper plate halves with green leaves. Insert the paper plate halves in the slits in the brown cardboard tubes to complete the trees. Make as many Arbor Day trees as desired. Let the children "plant" them all over the room.

316 Columbus Day Ships

Put a small piece of playdough in a walnut shell half. Decorate a small square of white paper for a sail and attach it to a toothpick. Stick the toothpick into the playdough. Make three ships for sailing in the water table on Columbus Day.

317 Groundhog Day Puppet

Cut a groundhog face (about 1½ inches in diameter) out of brown construction paper. Add facial features as desired. Attach the groundhog face to the top of a Popsicle stick. Cut a slit in the bottom of a small paper cup. Push the bottom of the Popsicle stick down through the slit in the cup. Then move the Popsicle stick up and down to make the groundhog appear and disappear.

318 Labor Day Hat Box

Collect hats from different occupations (construction worker, firefighter, chef, baseball player, clown, etc.) and put them in a special occupation hat box. Let the children take turns selecting a hat from the box and acting out what a person who wears that kind of hat does.

319 Liberty Bell Ring

Hang a bell up high. Let the children take turns tossing beanbags or rolled-up socks at the bell to make it ring.

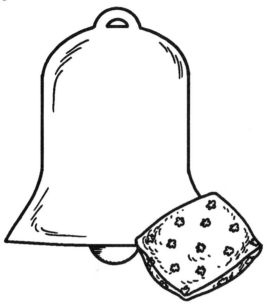

320 May Day Circle Basket

Cut two circles out of construction paper. Decorate the circles as desired. Fold the circles in half and staple them together as shown to make a basket. Complete the basket by stapling on a construction paper handle.

321 May Day Milk Carton Basket

Cut the top half off of any size of cardboard milk carton. Cover the carton with construction paper or self-stick paper. Decorate as desired and add a pipe cleaner handle.

322 Three-Cornered Hat

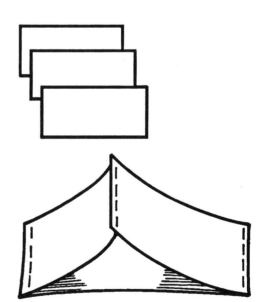

Cut a piece of 9- by 12-inch black construction paper into three 9- by 4-inch strips. Staple the short ends of the strips together as shown to complete the hat.

Instruments

Bells

323 **Bell Mitt**
Make a hand mitt out of felt or cotton fabric. Sew two bells onto the top. Have a child play the bell mitt by wearing it on one hand then clapping both hands together.

324 **Bell Pole**
Thread three or four bells together on a piece of string or yarn. Knot one end. Tape the other end to a dowel or other safe stick. Let a child play the bells by shaking the pole or tapping it with his or her hands.

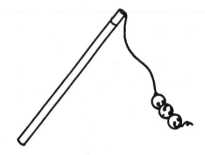

325 **Bell Shaker**

Tie a jingle bell in the middle of each of four pieces of string. Tie the strings tightly around a 12-inch dowel leaving 1 inch between each string.

326 **Jingle Pole**
Hammer a nail into the end of a 12-inch-long dowel or thin piece of wood, leaving a small space between the dowel and the head of the nail. Cut a 12-inch and an 8-inch length of yarn. Tie bells to the ends of the yarn pieces. Wrap the centers of the pieces of yarn around the nail. Hammer the nail into the dowel as far as it will go.

327 **Wrist Bells**
String three or four bells onto a large pipe cleaner. Twist the pipe cleaner around a child's wrist.

Blowing Instruments

328 **Bottle Blowers**
Fill one glass soft-drink bottle half full of water and another bottle three-quarters full of water. Let a child discover the different sounds the bottles make by blowing across their tops.

329 Cardboard Tube Kazoo

Attach a piece of waxed paper to one end of a cardboard toilet tissue tube with a rubber band. Make a hole near the other end of the tube with a nail or a hole punch. Let a child play the kazoo by humming into the open end of the tube.

330 Cardboard Tube Recorder

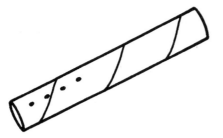

Poke holes near one end of a cardboard paper towel tube. Let a child play the recorder by humming through one end of the tube and covering and uncovering the holes with his or her fingers.

331 Trombone Bottle

Fill a glass bottle (a soft drink bottle works well) three-fourths full of water. Place a straw into the neck of the bottle. Have a child blow across the top of the straw while raising and lowering the bottle to create musical sounds.

Castanets

332 Bottle Cap Castanets

Use a hammer and a nail to punch two holes in each of two bottle caps. Thread a short piece of elastic string through the holes in each bottle cap and knot it. Let a child play the castanets by placing one on a thumb and one on a forefinger, then tapping them together.

333 Button Castanets

Thread a short piece of elastic string through the holes in each of two buttons. Let a child play the button castanets by placing one on a thumb and one on a forefinger, then tapping them together.

334 Cardboard Castanets

Cut out a 6- by 1½-inch piece of cardboard. Glue a small jar lid or bottle cap on each end. Fold the piece of cardboard in half. Let a child play the castanets by pressing the ends of the folded cardboard together. Small finger-grip holes can be cut into each side if the child finds the castanets difficult to manipulate.

335 | Jar Lid Castanets

Use a hammer and a nail to punch two holes in each of two jar lids. Thread a short piece of elastic string through the holes in each lid and knot it. Let a child play the lid castanets by placing one on a middle finger and one on a thumb, then tapping them together.

336 | Walnut Castanets

Select two walnut shell halves. Tape one shell, flat side out, on a child's thumb. Tape the other shell to the child's forefinger. Have the child play the walnut castanets by tapping them together.

Chimes

337 | Nail Chime

Tie ten or fifteen 6-inch pieces of string around a medium-sized embroidery hoop. Glue the strings to the hoop, leaving an equal space between each piece. Allow the glue to dry. Tie a medium-sized nail (no longer than 2½ inches) onto each string. Attach a long piece of yarn to the hoop to make a hanger. Let a child tap the nails with a metal object such as a table knife. Or hang the nail chime outside and let it blow and chime in the wind.

338 | Shell Chime

Tie several pieces of string around a cardboard tube, a dowel or a piece of driftwood, leaving a 1-inch space between each string. Tie three or four shells on each string, positioning them so they will hit each other when they are blown in the wind. Glue the shells in place. Attach a string hanger to the tube and hang it outside where it will blow in the wind.

339 | Silverware Chime

Gather several different sizes and kinds of silverware. Tie loops of string around the silverware handles. Thread the loops onto a long piece of rope. Tie the rope between two chairs or tables. Let a child hit the silverware with a metal spatula or spoon.

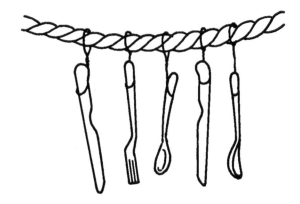

Cymbals

 Cookie Sheet Cymbals
Let the children bang small cookie sheets together. Or give them various kinds of metal objects such as a spatula, a serving spoon or a table knife to strike the cookie sheets with.

 Finger Cymbals
You will need two identical jar lids for each set of finger cymbals. Baby food jar lids work well. Using a nail and a hammer, make two holes through each lid. Then poke pipe cleaner pieces through the holes and twist them to make finger-sized handles. Have a child play the cymbals by placing one on a finger on each hand and striking them together.

 Frying Pan Cymbals
Let a child bang two frying pans together. Or give the child a large metal serving spoon and let him or her strike the edge of one pan with the spoon.

 Metal Pan Cymbals
Have the children bang metal pans or serving trays together.

 Pie Pan Cymbals
Nail a wooden block or knob onto a metal or aluminum pie pan to make a cymbal. Or poke two holes in an aluminum pie pan, insert pipe cleaners into the holes and twist them to make handles for the cymbals. Make two of each cymbal and let the children play them by striking the pie pans together.

Saucepan Lid Cymbals
Let a child hold the lid of a saucepan by the knob and strike the edge with a wooden or metal spoon. Or give the child two pot lids and let him or her bang them together.

Drums

346 Bongo Drums

Collect two or three round oatmeal boxes with lids. Put the lids on the boxes and tape them in place. Then fasten all the boxes together. Give the bongo drums to a child. Have the child sit down, place the drums on the floor and use his or her hands to beat out a rhythm on them.

347 Box Drums

Gather an assortment of boxes for drums, such as large and small gift boxes, shoeboxes, heavy cardboard boxes and cigar boxes. Tape the boxes securely shut. Store them in a large, open container in the music area. Let the children experiment with the different sounds each box drum makes.

348 Bucket Drum

Stretch heavy paper, cloth or plastic wrap tightly over the top of a bucket and secure it with string or tape. Let a child play the drum by beating the top of it with a wooden or plastic spoon.

349 Coffee Can Drum

Select a coffee can with a plastic lid. Punch two holes in opposite sides of the can near the top. String a piece of ribbon through the holes and tie the ends together. Put on the plastic lid. Have a child hang the drum around his or her neck and beat on it with his or her hands.

350 Pot And Pan Drums

Let the children use wooden spoons to hit the bottoms of assorted metal pots and pans.

Mallets

351 Bead Mallet

Wedge a wooden bead onto the end of an unsharpened pencil. If the bead is too large, wrap tape around the pencil until the bead fits snugly when slipped on.

352 Foam Mallet

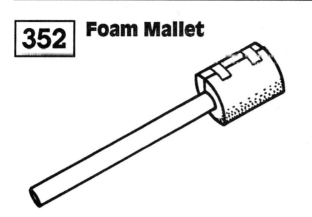

Tape a piece of foam around the end of a dowel or an unsharpened pencil.

353 Rubber Ball Mallet

Use a craft knife to make a hole in a solid rubber ball. Glue the end of a dowel in the hole. Allow the glue to dry.

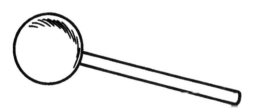

354 Rubber Tip Mallet

Collect a rubber tip from a chair or cane. Wedge the tip onto the end of a dowel. If the dowel is too small, wrap tape around it until the rubber tip fits snugly when put on.

Rhythm Sticks

355 Paper Rhythm Sticks

Make two rhythm sticks by rolling two 8½- by 11-inch pieces of paper into long tubes. Secure the papers with tape. Give them to a child and let him or her tap or rub them together to make sounds.

356 Rhythm Sticks

For each child collect two cardboard paper towel tubes, two wooden spoons or two wooden dowels. Let the children play the rhythm sticks by rubbing or tapping them together.

357 Sandpaper Rhythm Sticks

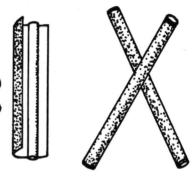

Collect two dowels for each child. Cut a piece of sandpaper to fit around each of the dowels. Wrap the sandpaper around the dowels and glue the edges in place. Use thumbtacks to secure the edges, if necessary. To make sounds, have the children rub the dowels together.

Shakers

358 Balloon Shaker

Place a teaspoon of rice, sand or dried beans into a deflated balloon. Blow up the balloon and tie a knot at the end.

359 Box Shaker

Fill a small gift box with dried beans, rice, popcorn kernels, bells, pebbles, sand, bottle caps, erasers or paper clips. Tape the lid closed.

360 Cardboard Tube Shaker

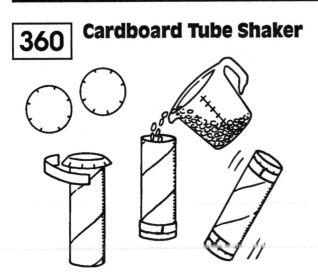

Cut two 2-inch circles out of construction paper. Make notches around the edges of the circles. Place one of the circles over one end of a cardboard toilet tissue paper tube, bend the notched edges down and tape them in place. Pour ¼ cup rice into the tube. Complete the shaker by taping the other circle onto the open end of the tube.

361 Cylinder Shaker

Collect a cylindrical container such as an oatmeal box or a coffee can. Fill the container with such things as rice, dried beans or popcorn kernels. Put on the lid and tape it securely closed.

362 Lemon Maraca

Remove the plug from a plastic lemon-shaped juice container. Rinse out the container and let it dry. Then put some rice inside of it. Insert a large unsharpened pencil or the handle of a wooden spoon into the neck of the container and tape it securely in place. Give the lemon maraca to a child and let him or her play it by shaking it back and forth.

363 Metal Box Shaker

Find a metal box with an attached lid, like the kind plastic bandages come in. Put two bells, some paper clips, some rice or a key inside of the box and tape the lid closed. Decorate the box with stickers. Give the box to a child and let him or her make sounds with it by shaking it back and forth.

364 Paper Bag Shaker

Fill a small paper bag with popcorn kernels, rice or dried beans. Decorate the bag with crayons or felt-tip markers. Securely tape the bag closed.

365 Paper Cup Shaker

Put some dried beans or rice in a paper cup. Place another paper cup upside down on top of it and tape the rims together. Decorate the shaker by attaching small crepe paper streamers to each end.

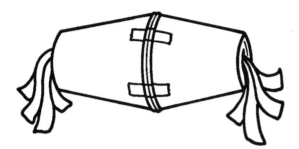

366 Paper Plate Shaker

Partially fill a small reclosable plastic bag with popcorn kernels or dried beans. Place the bag on the bottom half of a paper plate. Glue or staple a tongue depressor handle to the bottom of the plate. Then fold the top half of the plate over the plastic bag and tongue depressor and staple the open edges closed. Decorate the shaker as desired.

367 Pie Pan Shaker

Place one or two small scoops of rice, dried beans, dried peas or popcorn kernels into a disposable aluminum pie pan. Cover with another pie pan and staple the edges together. Let a child shake the pie pans tambourine style or strike the pan with his or her hands. The shaker can be decorated with ribbon or crepe paper streamers.

368 Plastic Egg Shaker

Fill plastic eggs with buttons or dried beans. Tape the halves together.

369 Plastic Jar Shaker

Select a clean plastic jar with a lid. Place two metal lids in the jar. Put glue around the rim of the jar and tightly screw on the lid. Give the shaker to a child and let him or her shake it all around to make sounds.

370 Soup Can Shaker

Put ¼ cup popcorn kernels into a clean empty soup can. Place another clean empty soup can upside down on top of it and tape the rims together.

371 Tennis Ball Shaker
Hold a tennis ball firmly and use a craft knife to make a ½-inch slit in one side. Squeeze the ball to open the slit and stuff in a few dried beans. The dried beans will not come out if it was difficult for you to get them into the ball.

Stringed Instruments

372 Chair Harp
Select a straight-backed chair with openings in the back rest. Collect several very large rubber bands or make your own by cutting strips from an inner tube. Stretch the rubber bands over the back of the chair. Let the children sit behind the chair and strum their hands across the rubber bands.

373 Ear Harp
Wrap rubber bands around a jar lid as shown in the illustration. If nessary, put tape over any sharp edges on the lid. Let a child hold the ear harp up to his or her ear and pluck the rubber band strings.

374 Milk Carton Banjo
Rinse and dry a half-gallon cardboard milk carton. Tape the top closed. Cut a rectangle in one side. Wrap the carton with four or five large rubber bands. Let a child play the banjo by strumming the rubber band "strings."

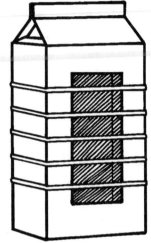

375 Rubber Band Strummer

Evenly space several rubber bands of different widths and sizes around a cigar box, a gift box lid or a candy-tin lid. Let the child play the instrument by strumming his or her fingers across the rubber bands guitar-style.

Tambourines

 ## Hoop Tambourine

Poke holes in the centers of six or seven bottle caps and string them onto a thin piece of wire. Stretch the wire across the middle of an embroidery hoop and wrap the ends around it. Secure the ends with tape to prevent them from slipping. Play the tambourine by shaking it or by holding it in one hand and tapping it against the palm of the other hand.

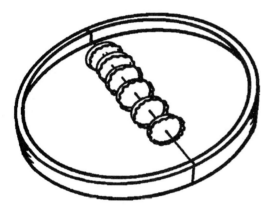

 ## Jingle Bell Tambourine

Tie a jingle bell in the middle of a 5-inch piece of string. Make five of these strings. Tie the strings to an embroidery hoop, leaving a space to hold onto the hoop. Secure the strings to the hoop with glue.

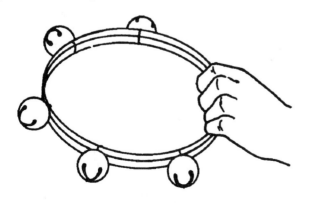

 ## Pie Pan Tambourine

Place two aluminum pie pans together, insides facing. Poke holes around the rims of the pie pans with a nail. Weave a long piece of string in and out of the holes to attach the pans together. Use a hammer and a nail to poke holes in the centers of bottle caps. Cut string into 5-inch lengths. Thread three bottle caps onto each piece of string. Then tie one string through each hole in the pie pans.

 ## Stick Tambourine

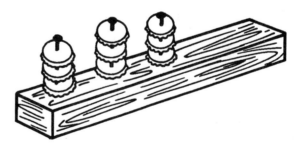

Find a thin straight piece of wood, 1 to 2 inches thick. Stack two or three bottle caps on top of each other and set them on top of the stick near one end. Hammer a nail through the bottle caps to secure them to the stick. Repeat two or three times. Make sure the nails do not poke out the other side. Let a child shake the stick or tap the un-nailed side against his or her palm.

380 Coat Hanger Triangle

Tie a string around the top of a wire coat hanger. Let a child hold the hanger by the string and strike it with a spoon.

381 Horseshoe Triangle

Tie a yarn or string handle around the top of a horseshoe. Let a child hold the horseshoe triangle by the yarn handle and strike it with a metal spoon.

382 Shelf Bracket Triangle

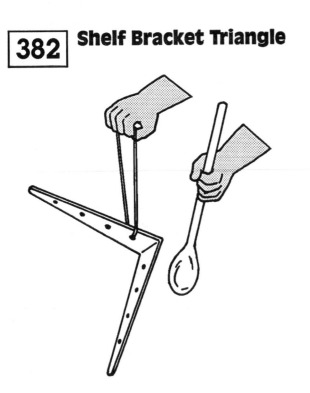

String some yarn through one of the holes in a metal L-shaped shelf bracket. (Metal shelf brackets are available at hardware stores.) Let a child hold the shelf-bracket triangle by the yarn handle and strike it with a metal spoon.

383 Cardboard Washboard

Cut a large square out of corrugated cardboard. Make sure one of the sides has the ridges exposed. Have a child scrape along the ridges with the edge of a spoon or a table knife.

384 Pie Pan Washboard

Let a child scrape along the edge of a disposable aluminum pie pan with a fingernail, a thimble or the edge of a metal spoon.

385 Clickers

Thread five or six buttons onto a 6-inch piece of string. Make a large knot at each end of the string so the buttons will not fall off. Have a child hold the string by the knots and lift one end, then the other, letting the buttons slide back and forth and click against one another. Use plastic, wooden or metal buttons for different kinds of sounds.

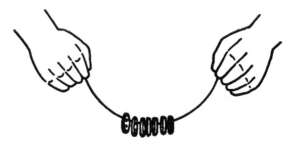

386 Coconut Clappers

Using a saw, cut about ½ of the way into a coconut. When the milk starts to drain out, pour it into a bowl. Finish cutting the coconut in half. Bake the coconut halves at 200 degrees for 20 minutes, if desired, to make the meat easier to remove. Scrape out the coconut meat with a table knife. Give the coconut halves to a child and show him or her how to clap the cut ends together.

387 Musical Jars

Fill several jars with different amounts of water. Line up the jars on a tabletop. Let a child tap the jars with a spoon and listen to the different sound each jar makes.

388 Sandpaper Blocks

Find two wood blocks of similar size. For each block cut out a piece of sandpaper to fit around four sides. Fasten the sandpaper to the blocks with glue, masking tape or nails. Give the blocks to a child and let him or her rub them together to make sounds.

389 Sandpaper Hands

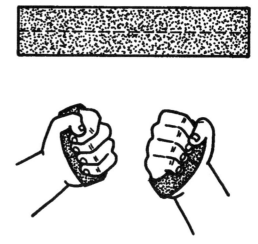

Fold a 2- by 10-inch piece of sandpaper in half the long way and cut it on the fold. Wrap a strip of the sandpaper around each of a child's hands. Show the child how to hold the sandpaper pieces in place with his or her thumbs. Then have the child rub the sandpaper on the backs of his or her hands together to produce a scratching sound.

390 Spoon Clickers

Give each child two metal teaspoons. Show the children how to hold the spoons back to back. Let them hit the spoons against the palms of their hands to produce clicking sounds.

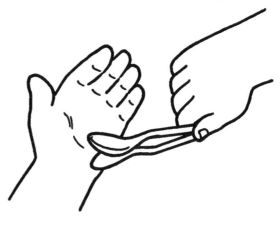

Learning Games

Color Games

391 Button Box

Divide a small box into four or more sections. Put a different color of construction paper in the bottom of each section. Give a child three or four buttons in each of the different colors. Let the child place the buttons in the matching colored sections.

392 Color Concentration

Cut two small squares out of each of several different colors of construction paper. Glue them to squares cut from index cards. Mix up the squares and place them color side down on a tabletop. Let a child turn over two to try to make a match. If the squares match, have the child remove the squares from the table. If the squares do not match, have the child turn the squares face down and let the next child try to make a match.

393 Color Objects

Paint each of six small boxes a different color. Let the children find small objects around the room and put them into the appropriate colored boxes.

394 Felt Color Matching Game

Cut several 4-inch squares from various colors of felt. Collect small colored toys, one to correspond with each color of felt. Set out the felt squares and let the children place the appropriate colored toy on each square. Store the toys and felt pieces in a shoebox or reclosable plastic bag.

Counting Games

395 Clothesline Counter

Use brightly colored felt-tip markers to color several spring-type clothespins. String a clothesline between two chairs at the children's eye level. Let the children place the clothespins on the clothesline. Then have them count all of the blue clothespins, all of the red clothespins, etc.

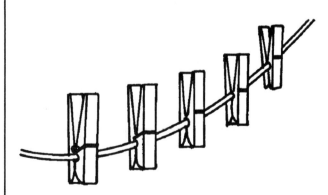

396 Clothespin Counting Wheel

Cut a large circle out of posterboard. Draw lines to divide the circle into four, eight or twelve sections. Print the numeral that represents the number of sections on the back of the wheel. Let the children place a spring-type clothespin onto each section of the wheel. Then have them count the number of clothespins and look on the back of the wheel to see if they counted correctly.

397 Clothespin Fingers

Cut two mitt shapes out of posterboard. Give the children ten clothespins. Let them clip the clothespins onto the mitt shapes to make fingers. Have them count the clothespin fingers and then their own fingers.

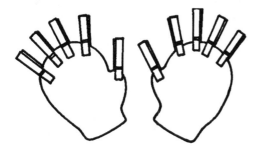

398 Nail Board

Make a nail board for the children to use while they are counting spools or wooden beads. Hammer long, small-headed nails into a square piece of wood. Space the nails 2 inches apart. Let the children place the spools or wooden beads onto the nails as they count them.

399 Number Line

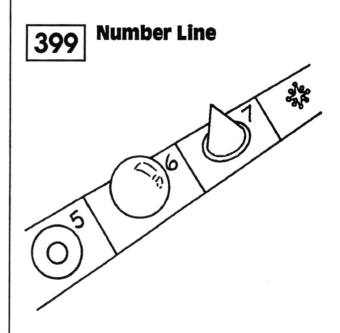

Tape together strips of posterboard to make a long number line. Mark off twenty sections and number them. Let the children set a block or other toy in each section. Ask them questions such as these: "What number is the round, red block on? What toy is on number seven? Where is the green truck?"

Five Senses Games

400 Feelie Box

Cut a hole large enough for a child's hand out of one end of a shoebox. Place an object inside of the box and put the lid on. Have the child put his or her hand through the hole in the box, feel the object and try to guess what it is. After the child guesses correctly, put a new item in the box and let another child have a turn.

401 Feelie Squares

Cut two squares out of each of several different textured fabrics. Use such fabrics as silk, flannel, lace, corduroy, terry cloth and fake fur. Set out the squares. Blindfold one child at a time and have him or her try to find the matching squares by touch.

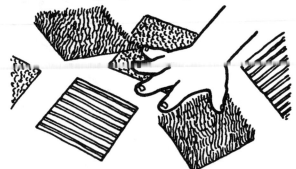

402 Hard And Soft Box

Fill a box with a variety of hard and soft objects. Use such hard objects as a block, a marble, a coin, a crayon, an empty spool and a rock. Use such soft objects as a cotton ball, a piece of fabric, a sponge, a piece of playdough and a stuffed animal. Have the children empty the objects out on the floor or a table. Then let them sort the items into two piles.

403 Listening Game

Collect eight small opaque plastic bottles with lids. Fill two bottles with beans, two with rice, two with salt and two with flour. Tape on the lids and mix up the bottles. Let the children shake the bottles to find the matching ones.

404 Sniffing Jars

You will need six small jars, six cotton balls and three fragrances such as perfume, onion juice and lemon juice. Put each fragrance on two of the cotton balls. Then place a cotton ball in each of the jars. Let the children sniff all of the jars and try to find the ones with the matching scents.

405 Texture Book

Cut 5- by 8-inch pieces out of cardboard. Poke holes along one of the 8-inch sides of each piece. Place the pieces on top of one another and lace string or yarn through the holes to make a book. On each page of the book, write a different texture word such as "Soft," "Rough," "Smooth," "Hard" or "Bumpy." Glue on a textured piece of material to show that texture. Then draw a simple picture of something with that texture. For example, if the texture word is "Rough," you could glue on a small piece of sandpaper and draw a picture of a brick wall. Let the children "read" the book by describing the textures on the pages. Ask them to name other items that have the same textures as those in the book.

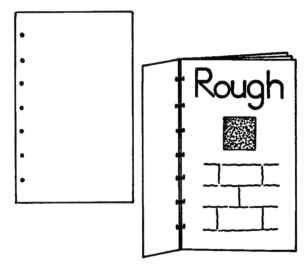

Letter Recognition Games

406 ABC Scrapbook

Use a scrapbook to create your own ABC picture book. Cut alphabet letters out of sandpaper or flocked wallpaper and glue one letter on each page. Then glue on a picture of something whose name begins with that letter. (Use pictures cut from magazines or coloring books.) Let the children take turns looking through the book, touching the textured letters and naming the pictures.

407 Accordion Book

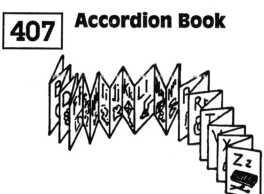

Fold thirteen large index cards in half. Unfold the cards and tape them together end to end. (Tape both sides of the cards for a more durable book.) Label the sections on the cards from "A" to "Z." On each section glue a small picture of something whose name begins with the letter that is printed on it. Fold the cards together accordion style. Use the book for "reading" at circle time or stand it on a low shelf or table for the children to look at.

408 Alphabet Block Match

Print letters or simple words on index cards. Place the cards and a set of alphabet blocks on a table. Let the children select cards and find alphabet blocks that match the letters on the cards.

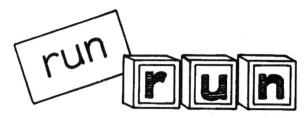

409 Alphabet Clothesline

Tie a clothesline between two chairs and clip on 26 clothespins. Cut 26 small clothing shapes out of construction paper. Label the shapes from "A" to "Z" and place them in a basket. Let the children take turns choosing a clothing shape, naming the letter on it and clipping it to the clothesline. Continue until each child has had a turn or until all the shapes have been hung on the line.

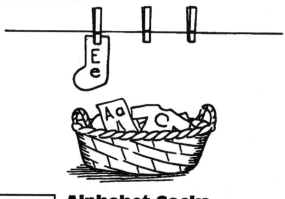

410 Alphabet Socks

Collect old unmatched socks. Label the socks with embroidered or ironed-on letters. Put the socks in a laundry basket. Let the children hang the socks on a clothesline, naming the letters as they go along.

411 Alpha-Match Puzzles

Use 8- by 10-inch posterboard rectangles to make puzzles for the letters of the alphabet. To make each puzzle, cut each rectangle into three puzzle pieces. Use a felt-tip marker to print an upper-case letter on the left-hand piece and a matching lower-case letter on the right-hand piece. On the middle piece draw a picture of something that begins with the printed letter. Set out the pieces of several puzzles at a time and let the children have fun putting them together.

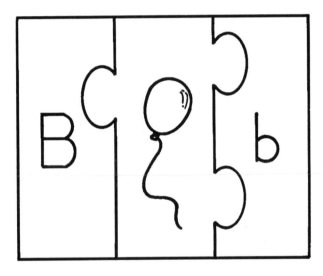

412 Letter Notebook

Make a notebook by punching holes in the tops of 27 index cards and inserting small metal rings. Use felt-tip markers to print "Letter Notebook" on the first card. Then starting with "A", print an upper- and lower-case letter of the alphabet on each of the remaining cards. Let the children turn the pages of the notebook, naming the letters and tracing over them with their fingers.

413 Net Letter Holder

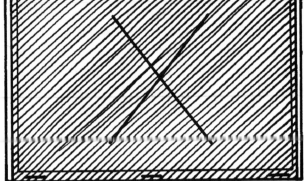

Staple nylon netting to a 4- by 6-inch index card along the two long edges, leaving the sides open. Print alphabet letters on slightly smaller cards. Slip one card at a time under the netting. Let the children trace the letter over the netting with their fingers while saying the letter's name.

414 Texture Letters

Cut letters out of posterboard. Glue a textured material such as yarn, ribbon, rice, glitter, dried beans or buttons on each letter. Set out the letters and let the children feel them.

415 Touch And Match Letter Cards

Choose several letters you wish to review. For each letter cut out two small posterboard squares. Use a brush dipped into glue to print the letters on the two cards. Then sprinkle on sand. When the glue has dried, set out the cards. Let the children trace over the textured letters with their fingers to find the matching pairs.

Matching Games

416 Matching Tools

Use the following materials for matching and sorting games: labels from canned foods; brand names and logos cut from food boxes; picture postcards; matchbook covers (with matches removed); colorful travel brochures.

417 Object Matching

Trace around various objects, such as a key, a cookie cutter, a sponge, a block and a spool, on a piece of posterboard. Let the children match the real objects to the tracings on the posterboard.

418 Photo Matching

Take a photo of each child and put it in a hat or a paper bag. Let the children take turns drawing a photo from the hat, finding the child pictured in the photo and giving the photo to that child.

419 Wrapping Paper Matching Game

Cut two shapes out of each of several patterns of wrapping paper. Set out one set of shapes and let the children find matching shapes from the other set.

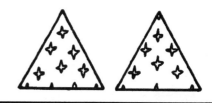

Math Games

420 Counting Fries

Cut a clean yellow sponge into long, skinny strips to use as "French fries." Let the children count how many fries will fit into a fast-food French fry holder.

421 Giant Die

Cover a large square cardboard box with solid-colored construction paper or self-stick paper. Make the box into a die by using a permanent black felt-tip marker to draw large dots representing the numbers 1 through 6 on its sides. Let the children toss the die into the air and count the number of dots on the side that comes up.

422 Magnetboard Counting

Place strips of masking tape on a metal cookie sheet. Let the children place small round magnets on the masking tape lines. Then have them count the number of magnets that fit on each line.

423 Math Strips
To make this game, you will need a 16-inch square of cardboard, a roll of self-stick magnetic tape and 55 round metal slugs. Cut a strip of magnetic tape that is long enough to hold one slug. Cut another strip to hold two slugs. Repeat, making strips to hold from three to ten slugs. Attach the magnetic strips to the cardboard. Give the children the board and the slugs. Let them put as many slugs as possible on each strip. Then have them count each strip's slugs.

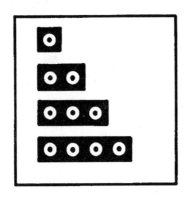

424 Pegboard Shape Outlines
Set out a piece of pegboard with any rough edges sanded or taped. Paint simple shape outlines on the board by "connecting the dots." Let the children place golf tees in the holes along the shape outlines.

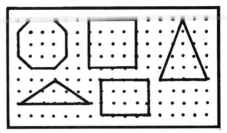

425 Pegboard Shapes
Set out pieces of pegboard with any rough edges sanded or taped. Let the children place golf tees in the holes of the pegboard to create shapes.

426 Rubber Band Design Board

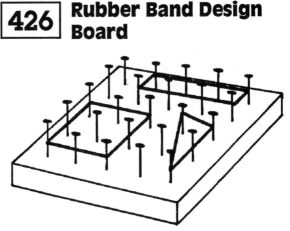

Hammer nails in a grid-like pattern, 1 inch apart, all over a plywood square. Give the board to a child along with a variety of different sizes and colors of rubber bands. Have the child stretch the rubber bands around the nails to create geometric shapes.

427 | Shape Pictures

Cut the following patterns out of cardboard: a large circle, a small circle, a large square, a small square, a large triangle, a small triangle, a large rectangle and a small rectangle. Use the patterns as guides to cut ten of each size and shape out of poster-board. Set all of the shapes on a table and let the children use them to create shape pictures.

428 | All Around the House

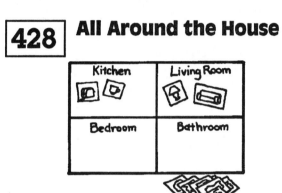

Divide a large piece of paper into four sections to make a simple floor plan. Label each section as a different room in a house, such as a kitchen, a bed-room, a living room and a bathroom. Cut out magazine pictures of objects you would find in each of the four rooms. Set out the floor plan and the magazine pictures. Have the children sort the pictures by placing them in the appropriate rooms.

429 | Boxes

Ask each child to bring in a small box. Place the boxes on a table. Let the children sort the boxes by shape, size, construction, former contents and color.

430 | All In a Row

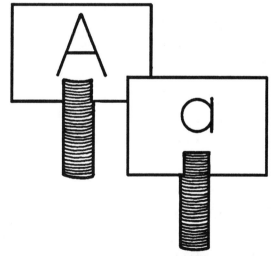

On three or four large index cards, draw the stages of an event that usu-ally happens in a series, one stage on each card. Select such events as grow-ing a pumpkin, making a cake or the seasons in a year. Mix up the cards and let the children arrange them in the proper order.

431 | Cardboard Tube Stands

Cover with felt or paint twelve to fifteen cardboard toilet tissue tubes. Cut a ½-inch slit on either side of one end of each tube. Use the tubes to hold learning game cards or shapes for counting or matching games.

432 Magnets

Collect a variety of freebie magnets (such as the ones with take-out pizza advertisements). Collect more than one of each kind, if possible. Use the magnets with a magnetboard for sorting, counting and matching games.

433 Paint Chip Sorting

Collect paint chip samples from a paint store or a home and garden store. Cut apart the shades on each paint strip and let the children put them in order from dark to light.

434 Picture Flaps

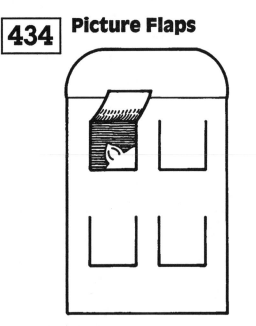

Cut four or five flaps in the front of a large manila envelope. Slide a picture inside the envelope facing forward. Open up one flap and let the children try to guess what the picture is. Continue opening the flaps, one at a time, until the children guess correctly. Then pull out the picture, show it to the children and replace it with another picture.

435 Poker Chips

Make a pattern with poker chips (two red, one blue, two red, one blue; one red, two blue, two white, one red, two blue, two white; etc.). Let the children repeat the pattern with other poker chips. Have younger children place the poker chips below the chips in the pattern, matching the colors. Let older children try to continue the pattern.

436 Snow Pals

From white posterboard cut three large circles, three medium circles and three small circles. Then cut out three black top hats. Have the children place all the large circles in a row. Let them place the medium circles on top of the large circles. Then have them place the small circles above the medium circles. Let the children add the top hats to make snow pals. Then mix up all the circles and hats and let the children make the snow pals all over again.

Multi-Usable
Learning Games

437 Basic Teaching Books

Make a book for each child by stapling four sheets of white paper together with a colored construction paper cover. Title the cover according to a selected learning concept ("Red Book," "Number Book," etc.). Let the children look through magazines and catalogs to find pictures that illustrate the learning concept. Then have them tear out the pictures and glue them in their books. (Let younger children choose from precut pictures that have been placed in a box.)

438 Beginning Sounds Books

Prepare teaching books as directed in prop 437, labeling the pages of the books with different alphabet letters. Then have the children glue pictures of things whose names begin with those letters on the appropriate pages in their books.

439 Classification Books

Prepare teaching books as directed in prop 437, choosing a subject such as foods and labeling the book pages "Breakfast," "Lunch" and "Dinner." Then have the children glue pictures of foods they usually eat for those meals on the appropriate pages in their books.

440 Color Books

Prepare teaching books as directed in prop 437, choosing a color such as red and making book covers out of red construction paper. Then have the children glue pictures of red things throughout their books. Or label the pages of the books with different colors and let the children glue on matching colored pictures.

441 Number Books

Prepare teaching books as directed in prop 437, numbering the pages of each book from 1 to 8. Then have the children glue pictures of one thing, pictures of two things, etc., on the corresponding numbered pages in their books.

442 Shape Books

Prepare teaching books as directed in prop 437, choosing a geometric shape such as a circle and having the children glue pictures of circular things throughout their books. Or label the pages of the books with different geometric shapes (circles, squares, triangles, etc.) and have the children glue on matching shaped pictures.

443 More Teaching Book Ideas

Prepare teaching books as directed in prop 437, using pictures of animals, toys, pets, etc. to make the corresponding books. Use textured materials (velvet, burlap, sandpaper, etc.) to make texture books. Use nature items (leaves, flowers, seeds, etc.) to make nature books.

444 Basic Teaching Buttons

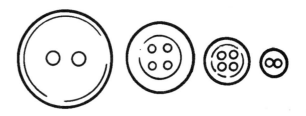
Provide buttons in a variety of colors, shapes, etc. Then let the children use the buttons to play sorting and matching games.

445 Color Buttons

Have the children sort buttons by color (use a muffin tin for a holder, if desired). Or lay out several different colored buttons and have the children place matching colored buttons next to them.

446 Number Buttons

Have the children count buttons by color, by shape or by size. Or lay out index cards with numerals written on them and have the children place corresponding numbers of buttons on the cards.

Shape Buttons

447 Have the children sort buttons by shape (round, square, flower-shaped, etc.). Or lay out several different shaped buttons and have the children place matching shaped buttons next to them.

448 **Size Buttons**

Have the children sort buttons by size (large, medium, small). Or lay out several different sized buttons and have the children place matching sized buttons next to them.

449 **Texture Buttons**

Have the children sort buttons by texture or by material. Or lay out several different textured buttons and have the children place matching textured buttons next to them.

450 **More Teaching Button Ideas**

Have the children sort buttons by number of holes. Use buttons to make math equations (two white buttons plus one black button, etc.). Lay out buttons in patterns (red, blue, red, blue; large, medium, small, large, medium, small; etc.).

451 **Basic Teaching Cards**

Use index cards to make a set of 12 game cards. On each set of four cards, draw pictures that are alike in some way (a red apple, a red car, a red horn, a red balloon, etc.). To play, lay out three cards containing pictures that are alike and one card containing a picture that is different. Then ask the children to identify the different picture and explain why it doesn't belong with the other three. Continue the game using combinations of the other cards.

452 **Animal Cards**

Prepare teaching cards as directed in prop 451, making four cards containing pictures of farm animals (a pig, a cow, etc.), four cards containing pictures of sea animals (a fish, an octopus, etc,) and four cards containing pictures of zoo animals (a tiger, an elephant, etc.).

453 Beginning Sounds Cards

Prepare teaching cards as directed in prop 451, making four cards containing pictures of things whose names begin with the "B" sound (a bear, a boat, etc.), four cards containing pictures of things whose names begin with the "C" sound (a cat, a cup, etc.) and four cards containing pictures of things whose names begin with the "D" sound (a dog, a doll, etc.).

454 Color Cards

Prepare teaching cards as directed in prop 451, making four cards containing red pictures, four cards containing yellow pictures and four cards containing blue pictures.

455 Number Cards

Prepare teaching cards as directed in prop 451, making four cards containing pictures of one object, four cards containing pictures of two objects and four cards containing pictures of three objects.

456 Shape Cards

Prepare teaching cards as directed in prop 451, making four cards containing pictures of round objects (a ball, a clock face, etc.), four cards containing pictures of square objects (a box, an alphabet block, etc.) and four cards containing pictures of triangular objects (a clown hat, a tepee, etc.).

457 More Teaching Card Ideas

Prepare teaching cards as directed in prop 451, making cards containing pictures of foods (fruits, vegetables, meats); pictures of vehicles (land, sea, air); etc. Use the cards to play sorting games (red pictures in one pile, yellow pictures in another pile, etc.).

Basic Teaching Clips

Make a set of clips by gluing two clothespins 2½ inches apart on a tongue depressor so that the clip ends of the clothespins are hanging down. To make each pair of game cards, fold a small index card in half and draw matching shapes, alphabet letters, etc., on the two halves. Draw a small star in the upper left-hand corner of the index card and another small star in the upper right-hand corner. Turn the card over and draw a large shape (any kind) in the center of the back. Then cut the card in half along the fold. Follow the same procedure to make a set of matching cards for each selected learning concept. To play, have the children clip matching cards to the clothespins with the stars in the upper left- and right-hand corners. If the matches are correct, the shapes drawn on the backs of the cards will fit together like puzzles.

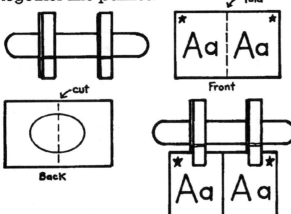

459 **Alphabet Clips**

Prepare teaching clips as directed in prop 458, writing a different upper-case letter on one half of each index card and a corresponding lower-case letter on the other half.

460 **Beginning Sounds Clips**

Prepare teaching clips as directed in prop 458, writing a different alphabet letter on one half of each index card and drawing a picture of something whose name begins with that letter on the other half.

461 **Color Clips**

Prepare teaching clips as directed in prop 458, drawing a different colored circle on one half of each index card and a matching colored circle on the other half. Or write a different color word ("Red," "Blue," etc.) on one half of each index card and draw a matching colored circle on the other half.

462 **Number Clips**

Prepare teaching clips as directed in prop 458, writing a different numeral on one half of each index card and drawing a corresponding number of dots or small pictures on the other half.

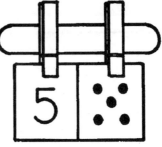

463 Shape Clips

Prepare teaching clips as directed in prop 458, drawing a different geometric shape (a circle, a square, a triangle, etc.) on one half of each index card and a matching geometric shape or shape picture (a ball, a box, a clown hat, etc.) on the other half.

464 More Teaching Clip Ideas

Prepare teaching clips as directed in prop 458, matching squares of patterned wallpaper or wrapping paper; pieces of textured materials (velvet, burlap, sandpaper, etc.); picture stickers; and pictures of animals, foods, articles of clothing, etc.

Teaching Clothesline

465 Basic Teaching Clothesline

Hang a length of clothesline between two chairs and clip clothespins onto the line. Cut clothing shapes (shirts, pants, socks, etc.) out of fabric and place them in a basket. Then let the children take turns "hanging up the wash" as you give directions.

466 Clothing Clothesline

Prepare clothing shapes and a teaching clothesline as directed in prop 465. Ask the children to hang up just the socks, just the dresses, etc. Or ask them to hang the pants on one side of the line and the shirts on the other side, etc.

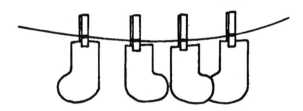

467 Color Clothesline

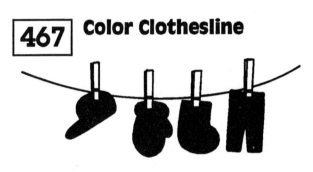

Hang a length of clothesline between two chairs and clip clothespins onto the line. Cut clothing shapes out of different colors of fabric. Ask the children to hang up just the green clothes, just the yellow clothes, etc. Or hang different colored clothing shapes on the line and ask the children to hang matching colored shapes next to them.

468 Number Clothesline

Prepare clothing shapes and a teaching clothesline as directed in prop 564. Ask the children to hang up five clothing shapes, three clothing shapes, etc. Or ask them to hang up two shirts and one dress, etc., and then tell how many shapes there are all together.

469 Pattern Clothesline

Prepare clothing shapes and a teaching clothesline as directed in prop 465. Ask the children to hang up the wash in patterns (red, blue, red, blue; circle, square, circle, square; pants, shirt, sock, pants, shirt, sock; etc.).

470 Shape Clothesline

Hang a length of clothesline between two chairs and clip clothespins onto the line. Cut geometric shapes (circles, squares, triangles, etc.) out of fabric. Ask the children to hang up just the triangles, just the circles, etc. Or hang different geometric shapes on the line and ask the children to hang matching shapes next to them.

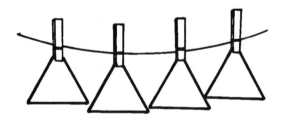

471 More Teaching Clothesline Ideas

Hang a length of clothesline between two chairs and clip clothespins onto the line. Ask the children to hang up pairs of clothing shapes cut from matching patterned fabric (striped, checked, flowered, etc.); or clothing shapes cut from matching textured fabric (velvet, satin, corduroy, etc.).

Teaching Crowns

472 Basic Teaching Crowns

Cut crown shapes out of large sheets of construction paper. Have the children glue pictures, shapes, etc. on their crowns. Then tape the ends of each crown together in the back.

473 Color Crowns

Choose a color such as red and make crowns out of red construction paper. Let the children look through magazines to find red pictures. Then have them tear out the pictures and glue them on their crowns. (Let younger children choose from precut pictures that have been placed in a box.)

474 Holiday Crowns

Choose appropriate colored construction paper to make crowns and shapes for each holiday (red and pink for Valentine's Day, orange and black for Halloween, etc.). Cut out holiday shapes (bears, pumpkins, etc.) in a variety of sizes and let the children glue them on their crowns.

475 | Number Crowns

Cut crown shapes out of large sheets of construction paper. On the front of each crown, write a numeral such as "3." Then let the children glue different sets of three items (three buttons, three stickers, etc.) on their crowns.

476 | Shape Crowns

Cut crown shapes out of large sheets of construction paper. Choose a geometric shape, such as a triangle. Cut various colors and sizes of triangles out of construction paper and let the children glue them on their crowns.

477 | Texture Crowns

Cut crown shapes out of large sheets of construction paper. Cut different kinds of textured materials into small pieces. Then let the children glue combinations of rough and smooth textured materials on their crowns.

478 | More Teaching Crown Ideas

Cut crown shapes out of large sheets of construction paper. Use magazine pictures to make animal crowns, food crowns, transportation crowns, etc. Use actual items to make leaf crowns, shell crowns, seed crowns, etc.

Teaching Cubes

479 | Basic Teaching Cube

Cut index cards to fit in the sides of photo cubes. Draw pictures, shapes, etc., on the cards and insert them in the cubes. Then let the children use the cubes to play various kinds of learning games.

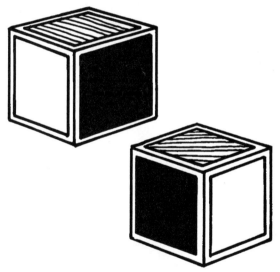

480 | Color Cubes

Prepare teaching cubes as directed in prop 479, putting different colored cards in the sides of one photo cube and matching colored cards in the sides of another photo cube in a different order. Then let the children move the cubes around to find the matching pairs of colors.

481 | Dice Cubes

Prepare teaching cubes as directed in prop 479, putting cards containing different numerals from 1 to 6 in the sides of two photo cubes. Let the children use the dice when playing games. For example, tape construction paper circles to the floor to make "stepping stones" for a start-to-finish game. Let the children take turns rolling a die, naming the number that comes up and then taking that number of steps toward the finish line.

482 | Number Cubes

Prepare teaching cubes as directed in prop 479, putting cards containing different numerals in the sides of one photo cube and cards containing corresponding numbers of dots or small pictures in the sides of another photo cube in a different order. Then let the children move the cubes around to find the matching pairs of numbers.

483 | Sequence Cubes

Prepare teaching cubes as directed in prop 479, putting cards containing pictures that illustrate a

sequence in the sides of three or four photo cubes (a seed in the ground, a sprout, a flower in blossom; a tree in spring, a tree in summer, a tree in fall, a tree in winter; etc.). Then let the children line up the photo cubes in the proper sequence.

484 | Shape Cubes

Prepare teaching cubes as directed in prop 479, putting cards containing different basic shapes (a circle, a square, a triangle, a star, etc.) in the sides of one photo cube and cards containing matching shapes in the sides of another photo cube in a different order. Then let the children move the cubes around to find the matching pairs of shapes.

485 | More Teaching Cube Ideas

Prepare teaching cubes as directed in prop 479, matching upper-case letters with corresponding lower-case letters; alphabet letters and pictures of things whose names begin with those letters; and pictures of animals, foods, vehicles, etc.

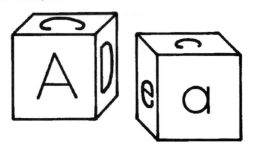

Teaching Cups

486 Basic Teaching Cups

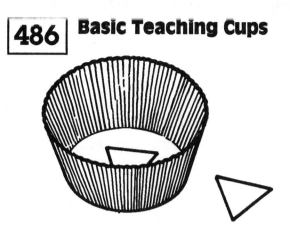

Draw shapes, numerals, etc., on the bottoms of six paper baking cups and place them in a muffin tin. Cut matching shapes out of construction paper or assemble the desired kind and number of small objects into the appropriate muffin tin cups. (An egg carton cut in half can be substituted for the muffin tin and cupcake liners.)

487 Classification Cups

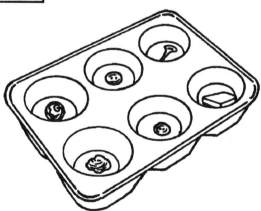

Place a different kind of small object in each cup of a muffin tin (a penny in one cup, a button in another cup, etc.). Provide the children with a box containing several of each kind of small object.

488 Color Cups

Color the bottom of each of six paper baking cups a different color. Put the baking cups in a muffin tin. Cut small matching colored circles out of construction paper or provide the children with matching colored buttons or beads.

489 Number Cups

Number the bottoms of six paper baking cups from 1 to 6 and place them in the cups of a muffin tin in random order. Provide the children with 21 buttons, beads, etc.

490 Picture Cups

Attach a different picture sticker to the bottom of each of six paper baking cups. Put the baking cups in a muffin tin. Attach matching picture stickers to small construction paper circles.

491 Shape Cups

Draw a different basic shape (a circle, a square, a triangle, a star, etc.) on the bottom of each of six paper baking cups. Put the baking cups in a muffin tin. Cut small matching shapes out of construction paper.

492 More Teaching Cup Ideas

Write upper-case letters on the bottoms of paper baking cups and corresponding lower-case letters on construction paper circles. Place circles of different patterned wallpaper or wrapping paper in the cups of a muffin tin and cut out matching patterned circles.

Teaching Dominoes

493 Basic Teaching Dominoes

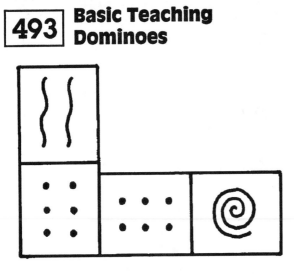

Cut posterboard or index cards into 21 small cards (about 1½ by 4 inches each). Divide each card in half with a line and draw a shape, a set of dots, etc., in each half. Give each child a number of cards and place the remaining cards face down in a pile. Let one child begin by placing a card in the middle of the playing area. If the next child has a card with a half that matches one of the halves of the first card, have the child place the card next to the first card so that the matching halves are touching (either vertically or horizontally). If the child does not have a matching card, let him or her draw cards from the pile until a match is found. Continue the game, letting the children match the cards any way they wish, until all the cards have been played.

494 Color Dominoes

Choose six colors such as red, yellow, blue, green, orange and purple. Draw two colored circles on each of 21 small cards, using these combinations: red-red, red-yellow, red-blue, red-green, red-orange, red-purple; yellow-yellow, yellow-blue, yellow-green, yellow-orange, yellow-purple; blue-blue, blue-green, blue-orange, blue-purple; green-green, green-orange, green-purple; orange-orange, orange-purple; purple-purple. Let the children use the cards as described in prop 493.

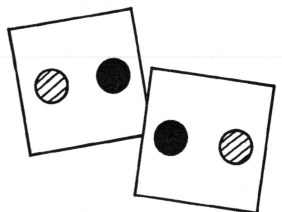

495 Number Dominoes

Choose six numbers such as 0, 1, 2, 3, 4 and 5. Draw two sets of dots to represent the numbers on each of 21 small cards (for 0, leave the cards blank). Use these combinations: 0-0, 0-1, 0-2, 0-3, 0-4, 0-5; 1-1, 1-2, 1-3, 1-4, 1-5; 2-2, 2-3, 2-4, 2-5; 3-3, 3-4, 3-5; 4-4, 4-5; 5-5. Let the children use the cards as described in prop 493.

496 Picture Dominoes

Choose six different picture stickers such as a bear, a flower, a cat, a rainbow, a duck and a clown (seven of each). Attach two stickers on each of 21 small cards, using these combinations: bear-bear, bear-flower, bear-cat, bear-rainbow, bear-duck, bear-clown; flower-flower, flower-cat, flower-rainbow, flower-duck, flower-clown; cat-cat, cat-rainbow, cat-duck, cat-clown; rainbow-rainbow, rainbow-duck, rainbow-clown; duck-duck, duck-clown, clown-clown. Let the children use the cards as described in prop 493.

497 Shape Dominoes

Choose six basic shapes such as a circle, a square, a triangle, a rectangle, a diamond and a star. Draw two shapes on each of 21 small cards, using these combinations: circle-circle, circle-square, circle-triangle, circle-rectangle, circle-diamond, circle-star; square-square, square-triangle, square-rectangle, square-diamond, square-star; triangle-triangle, triangle-rectangle, triangle-diamond, triangle-star; rectangle-rectangle, rectangle-diamond, rectangle-star; diamond-diamond, diamond-star; star-star. Let the children use the cards as described in prop 493.

Teaching Donuts

498 Basic Teaching Donuts

Cut an 18-inch circle out of posterboard. Go in 3 inches from the edge and cut out a smaller circle. Then go in 3 inches from the edge of the smaller circle and cut out a third circle. You will end up with two donuts and a small circle "pie," each of which can be made into a separate matching game. Use a felt-tip marker to divide the large donut into ten sections, the small donut into six sections and the pie into four sections. On opposite sides of each dividing line, attach matching stickers or write corresponding alphabet letters, etc. Cut out the sections and place them in three separate reclosable plastic bags. Then let the children piece together the donuts and the pie by matching the stickers, letters, etc., on the ends of the sections.

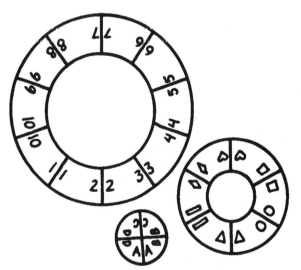

499 Alphabet Donuts

Prepare teaching donuts as directed in prop 498, writing a different upper-case letter on one side of each dividing line and a corresponding lower-case letter on the other side.

500 Color Donuts

Prepare teaching donuts as directed in prop 498, attaching a different colored sticker on one side of each dividing line and a matching colored sticker on the other side.

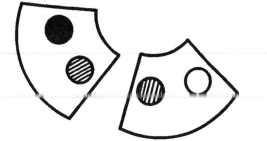

501 Number Donuts

Prepare teaching donuts as directed in prop 498, writing a different numeral on one side of each dividing line and attach a corresponding number of stickers on the other side.

502 Picture Donuts

Prepare teaching donuts as directed in prop 498, attaching a different picture sticker on one side of each dividing line and a matching picture sticker on the other side.

503 Shape Donuts

Prepare teaching donuts as directed in prop 498, attaching a sticker cut into a different basic shape (a circle, a square, a triangle, a star, etc.) on one side of each dividing line and a matching shaped sticker on the other side.

Teaching Fish

504 Basic Teaching Fish

Tie 3 feet of string to a paper towel tube, a wooden spoon, etc. Attach a magnet to the end of the string. Cut fish shapes out of construction paper and attach a paper clip to each fish. Then lay the shapes out on the floor and let the children take turns "catching fish" as you give directions.

505 Beginning Sounds Fish

Make a fishing pole as described in prop 504. Choose a sound such as the "H" sound. On fish shapes, draw pictures of things whose names begin with that sound (a house, a hat, etc.). On several other fish shapes, draw picture of things whose names begin with different sounds (a pig, a car, etc.). As the fish are caught, ask the children to name the pictures and tell whether or not the names begin with the chosen sound.

506 Color Fish

Make a fishing pole as described in prop 504. Cut fish shapes out of different colors of construction paper. Ask the children to catch just the red fish, just the yellow fish, etc.

507 Number Fish

Make a fishing pole as described in prop 504. Ask the children to catch five fish, three fish, etc. Or write numerals on the fish shapes and ask the children to catch a "two" fish, a "four" fish, etc.

508 Shape Fish

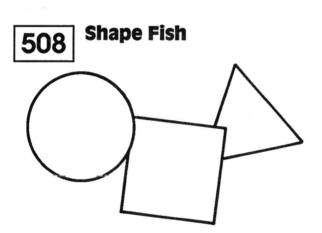

Make a fishing pole as described in prop 504. Cut geometric shapes (circles, squares, triangles, etc.) out of construction paper. Ask the children to catch just the circles, just the triangles, etc.

509 Size Fish

Make a fishing pole as described in prop 504. Cut out various sizes of fish shapes. Ask each child in turn to catch the largest fish, then the smallest. When all the fish have been caught, let the children sort them into piles of small fish, medium-sized fish and large fish.

510 More Teaching Fish Ideas

Make a fishing pole as described in prop 504. Write alphabet letters on fish shapes and catch "A" fish, "D" fish, etc. Draw different kinds of faces on fish shapes and catch happy fish, sad fish, sleepy fish, etc.

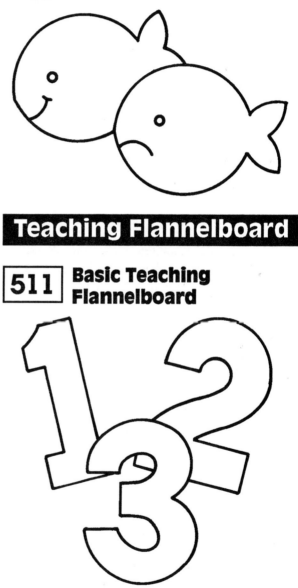

Teaching Flannelboard

511 Basic Teaching Flannelboard

Cut felt into shapes, numerals, etc. Cut pictures out of magazines or old books and back them with felt strips. Then let the children place the cutouts on a flannelboard as you give directions.

512 Beginning Sounds Flannelboard

Cut an alphabet letter such as "B" out of felt and place it on a flannelboard. Cut out pictures of things whose names begin with the "B" sound (a balloon, a ball, etc.) along with several pictures of things whose names begin with other sounds (a cat, a tree, etc.). Then ask the children to sort through the pictures and place those whose names begin with the "B" sound on the flannelboard.

513 Color Flannelboard

Cut shapes (fish, hearts, etc.) out of different colors of felt. Ask the children to place just the yellow shapes on a flannelboard, just the red shapes, etc. Or place different colored shapes on the flannelboard and ask the children to place matching colored shapes next to them.

514 Language Flannelboard

Cut pictures out of magazines or old books. Place the pictures on a flannelboard one at a time and let the children use them to make up a continuous story. Or let each child choose a picture, place it on the flannelboard and tell a few sentences about it.

515 Number Flannelboard

Cut the numerals 1 to 5 out of felt. Ask the children to line up the numerals on a flannelboard in the proper sequence. Or place sets of shapes (three stars, two diamonds, etc.) on the flannelboard and ask the children to place corresponding numerals next to them.

516 Shape Flannelboard

Cut geometric shapes (circles, squares, triangles, etc.) out of felt. Ask the children to place just the circles on a flannelboard and ask the children to place matching geometric shapes next to them.

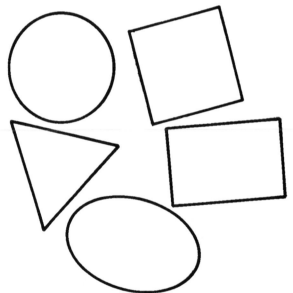

517 More Teaching Flannelboard Ideas

Cut out pictures that illustrate a sequence (a baby, a child, an adult; etc.) and put them in order on a flannelboard. Classify shapes or pictures by size (big and little). Place shapes or pictures on the flannelboard to reinforce concepts of over and under; top, bottom and middle; etc.

518 Basic Teaching Folders

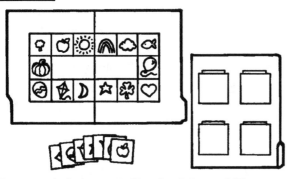

Draw pictures on the insides of file folders to make gameboards and cover them with clear self-stick paper. Make game cards by drawing matching pictures on posterboard or index cards, covering them with clear self-stick paper and then cutting them out. Tape squares of posterboard on the fronts of the file folders to make envelopes for holding the game cards. Then let the children use the folders to play matching and sorting games.

519 Alphabet Folders

Prepare teaching folders as directed in prop 518, drawing eight flowers, hearts, etc., on the insides of each file folder and writing a different upper-case letter inside each picture. Draw matching pictures that contain corresponding lower-case letters on posterboard and cut them out. Then let the children match the letters by placing the cutouts on top of the corresponding pictures on the file folders.

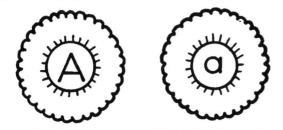

520 Color Folders

Prepare teaching folders as directed in prop 518, drawing eight different colored bears, stars, etc., on the insides of each file folder. Draw matching colored pictures on posterboard and cut them out. Then let the children match the colors by placing the cutouts on top of the corresponding pictures on the file folders.

521 Number Folders

Prepare teaching folders as directed in prop 518, drawing eight apples, suns, etc., on the insides of each file folder and writing a different numeral inside each picture. Draw matching pictures that contain corresponding numbers of dots on posterboard and cut them out. Then let the children match the numbers by placing the cutouts on top of the corresponding pictures on the file folders.

522 Shape Folders

Prepare teaching folders as directed in prop 518, drawing eight basic shapes (a circle, a square, a triangle, a star, etc.) on the insides of each file folder. Draw matching shapes on posterboard and cut them out. Then let the children match the shapes by placing the cutouts on top of the corresponding shapes on the file folders.

523 | Sorting Folders

Choose a subject such as animals and label one side of an open file folder "Farm" and the other side "Zoo" (or draw pictures to indicate the labels). Draw pictures of farm animals and zoo animals on posterboard and cut them out. Then let the children sort the pictures by placing them on the appropriate sides of the file folder.

524 | More Teaching Folders Ideas

Prepare teaching folders as directed in prop 518 for matching pictures of stickers or pictures cut from canned good labels, magazine ads, etc. Use sorting folders as described in prop 523 to sort pictures of shapes (circles-squares, etc.) or foods (fruits-vegetables, etc.).

Teaching Graph

525 | Basic Teaching Graph

On a large sheet of posterboard, draw lines to make an outline for a bar graph. Write the numerals 1 to 12 across the top of the outline. Cover the posterboard with clear self-stick paper. Then use the graph outline each day to record the results of a survey you take with the children. Choose a topic such as birthdays. Title the graph "Our Birthdays" and list the categories "Spring," "Summer," "Fall" and "Winter" (or draw pictures to indicate the categories). Count with the children how many of them have birthdays in spring, how many have birthdays in summer, etc. Then record

the numbers by drawing bars on the graph with crayons. Discuss the results of the survey. Ask questions such as these: "Which group is smaller, the one with birthdays in summer or the one with birthdays in winter? How many more have birthdays in spring than have birthdays in fall?" When you have finished, wipe the graph with a dry paper towel to remove the crayon.

526 | Color Graph

Use the teaching graph from prop 525. Title the graph "Our Shirts" and list categories such as "White," "Blue," "Green" and "Yellow." Have the children count how many of them are wearing white shirts, how many are wearing blue shirts, etc.

527 | Food Graph

Use the teaching graph from prop 525. Title the graph "Our Favorite Foods" and list categories such as "Chicken," "Corn," "Ice Cream" and "Watermelon." Count with the children how many of them like chicken the best, how many like corn the best, etc.

528 Number Graph

Use the teaching graph from prop 525. Title the graph "Our Brothers And Sisters" and list categories such as "None," "One," "Two," "Three" and "Four." Count with the children how many of them have no brothers or sisters, how many have one brother or sister, etc.

OUR BROTHERS AND SISTERS
1 2 3 4 5 6 7 8 9 10 11 12
None
One
Two
Three
Four

529 Shape Graph

Use the teaching graph from prop 525. Title the graph "Our Toys" and list categories such as "Round," "Square," "Triangular" and "Rectangular." Have the children count the number of round toys in the room, the number of square toys, etc.

530 More Teaching Graph Ideas

Use the teaching graph from prop 525. Choose topics to graph such as these: colors of hair (brown, black, etc.); numbers of riding toys (tricycles, wagons, etc.); kinds of shoes (tie-ons, strapons, etc.); favorite stories ("The Three Bears," "Little Red Riding Hood," etc.).

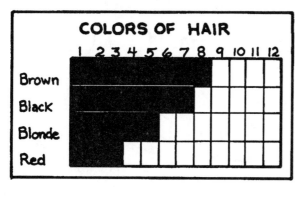

COLORS OF HAIR
1 2 3 4 5 6 7 8 9 10 11 12
Brown
Black
Blonde
Red

531 Basic Teaching Lotto

Cut posterboard into 9-inch squares to make gameboards. Divide each gameboard into nine squares and draw pictures, shapes, etc., in the squares. For each gameboard, make a set of nine matching game cards on 3-inch squares cut from posterboard. Tape large squares of posterboard on the backs of the gameboards to make envelopes for holding the game cards. Then let the children play matching games by placing the game cards on top of the corresponding squares on the gameboards.

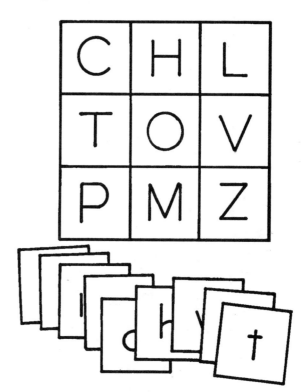

532 Alphabet Lotto

Divide a 9-inch square gameboard into nine squares. Write a different upper-case letter in each square. Write corresponding lower-case letters on nine 3-inch game cards.

533 Beginning Sounds Lotto

Divide a 9-inch gameboard into nine squares. Draw a picture of something whose name begins with a different sound in each square (a bee in one square, a fork in another square, etc.). Write the corresponding beginning alphabet letters on nine 3-inch game cards.

534 Color Lotto

Cut nine 3-inch squares out of different colors of construction paper and glue the squares on a 9-inch square gameboard. Cut matching 3-inch squares out of construction paper and glue them on the nine 3-inch square game cards.

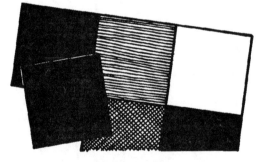

535 Number Lotto

Divide a 9-inch square gameboard into nine squares. Draw a different number of small pictures in each square (three balloons in one square, five flowers in another square, etc.). Write corresponding numerals on nine 3-inch square game cards.

536 Shape Lotto

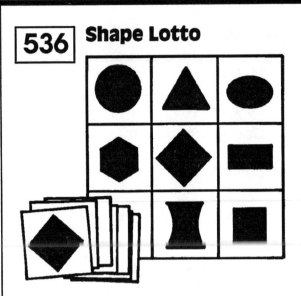

Divide a 9-inch square gameboard into nine squares. Draw a different basic shape (a circle, a square, a triangle, a star, etc.) in each square. Draw matching shapes on nine 3-inch game cards.

537 More Teaching Lotto Ideas

Make gameboards and cards as directed in prop 531 for matching pictures of animals, foods, vehicles, etc.; squares of patterned wallpaper or wrapping paper; squares of textured materials (velvet, burlap, sandpaper, etc.).

Teaching Magnetboard

538 | Basic Teaching Magnetboard

Cut shapes out of posterboard. Attach small magnets or strips of magnetic tape to the backs of the shapes. Then let the children place the shapes on a magnetboard as you give directions. (Shapes can also be made out of playdough and backed with small magnets.)

539 | Alphabet Magnetboard

Cut squares out of posterboard. Write upper-case letters on one set of squares and corresponding lower-case letters on another set. Attach small magnets or strips of magnetic tape to the backs of the squares. Place the upper-case letters on the magnetboard and ask the children to place the corresponding lower-case letters next to them. (Older children can use the letters to spell words.)

540 | Color Magnetboard

Cut shapes (bears, stars, etc.) out of different colors of posterboard. Attach small magnets or strips of magnetic tape to the backs of the shapes. Ask the children to place just the red shapes on the magnetboard, just the blue shapes, etc. Or place different colored shapes on the magnetboard and ask the children to place matching colored shapes next to them.

541 | Number Magnetboard

Cut five squares out of posterboard and number them from 1 to 5. Attach small magnets or strips of magnetic tape to the backs of the shapes. Ask the children to line up the numerals on the magnetboard in the proper sequence. Or place sets of shapes (two suns, five hearts, etc.) on the magnetboard and ask the children to place corresponding numerals next to them.

542 Picture Magnetboard

Cut various sizes of geometric shapes out of posterboard. Attach small magnets or strips of magnetic tape to the backs of the shapes. Then let the children put the shapes together on the magnetboard to create pictures of people, houses, robots, etc.

543 Shape Magnetboard

Cut geometric shapes (circles, squares, triangles, etc.) out of posterboard. Attach small magnets or strips of magnetic tape to the backs of the shapes. Ask the children to place just the squares on the magnetboard, just the triangles, etc. Or ask the children to place matching geometric shapes next to them.

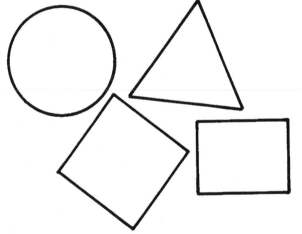

544 More Teaching Magnetboard Ideas

Cut various sizes and colors of shapes out of posterboard. Attach small magnets or strips of magnetic tape to the backs of the shapes. Use shapes to make math equations (two stars plus three circles, etc.); use shapes to make patterns (red, blue, red, blue; circle, square, triangle, circle, square, triangle; etc.).

Teaching Mailboxes

545 Basic Teaching Mailbox

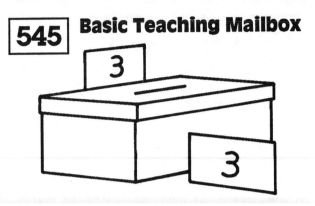

Make mailboxes by covering the lids of three or more shoeboxes with construction paper and cutting a slit in the top of each lid. Put the lids on the boxes. Draw shapes, alphabet letters, etc., on small index cards and tape them to the backs of the mailboxes so that they stand above the lids. Make "letters" for the mailboxes by drawing matching shapes, alphabet letters, etc., on the fronts of sealed envelopes. Then mix up the envelopes and let the children take turns "mailing" them through the slots of the appropriate mailboxes.

546 Alphabet Mailboxes

Prepare teaching mailboxes as described in prop 545, taping cards containing different upper-case letters to the backs of the mailboxes. Write corresponding lower-case letters on the fronts of the envelopes.

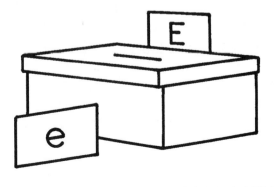

547 Color Mailboxes

Prepare teaching mailboxes as described in prop 545, taping different colored cards to the backs of the mailboxes. Draw matching colored circles or pictures on the fronts of the envelopes.

548 Feelings Mailboxes

Prepare teaching mailboxes as described in prop 545, taping cards containing different faces (happy, sad, sleepy, etc.) to the backs of the mailboxes. Draw matching faces on the fronts of the envelopes.

549 Number Mailboxes

Prepare teaching mailboxes as described in prop 545, taping cards containing different numerals to the backs of the mailboxes. Draw corresponding numbers of dots or small pictures on the fronts of the envelopes.

550 Shape Mailboxes

Prepare teaching mailboxes as described in prop 545, taping cards containing different basic shapes (a circle, a square, a triangle, a star, etc.) to the backs of the mailboxes. Draw matching shapes on the fronts of the envelopes.

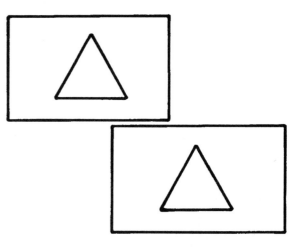

551 More Teaching Mailbox Ideas

Prepare teaching mailboxes as directed in prop 545 for matching alphabet letters with pictures of things whose names begin with those letters and for matching pictures of animals, foods, articles of clothing, etc.

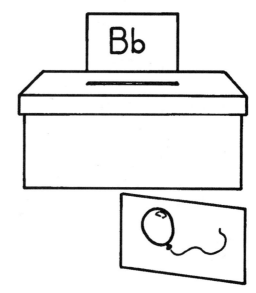

552 Basic Teaching Pegboard

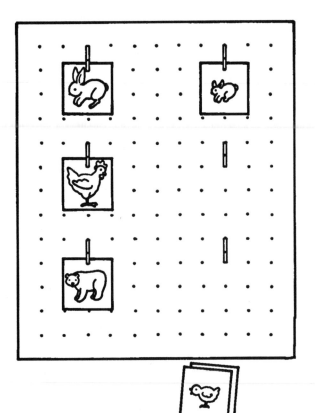

Hang peg hooks down a piece of pegboard in two parallel rows. Cut index cards in half. Draw shapes, alphabet letters, etc., on one set of cards and make another set of cards to match. Cover the cards with clear self-stick paper and punch a hole in the top of each card. Hang one set of cards on the peg hooks in the left-hand row. Then let the children hang matching cards from the second set on the appropriate peg hook in the right-hand row. (A wooden board with cup hooks screwed into it can be substituted for the pegboard and peg hooks.)

553 Alphabet Pegboard

Prepare a teaching pegboard as described in prop 552. Write different upper-case letters on one set of cards and corresponding lower-case letters on another set. Hang one set of cards on the peg hooks in the left-hand row. Then let the children hang the matching cards from the second set on the appropriate hooks in the right-hand row.

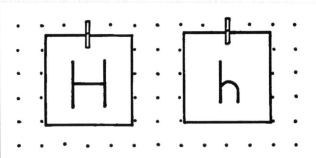

554 Beginning Sounds Pegboard

Prepare a teaching pegboard as described in prop 552. Write different alphabet letters on one set of cards and draw pictures of things whose names begin with those letters on another set. Hang one set of cards on the peg hooks in the left-hand row. Then let the children hang the matching cards from the second set on the appropriate hooks in the right-hand row.

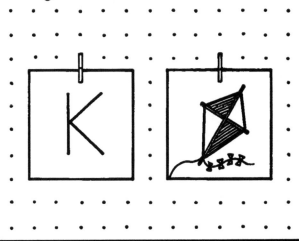

555 | Color Pegboard

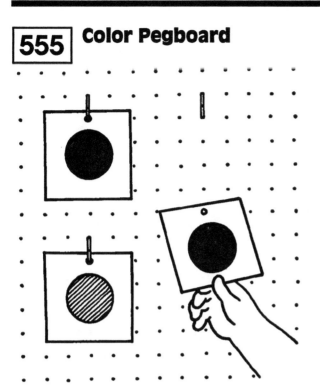

Prepare a teaching pegboard as described in prop 552. Draw different colored circles on one set of cards and matching colored circles on another set. Or draw different colored pictures on one set of cards and matching colored circles on another set. Hang one set of cards on the peg hooks in the left-hand row. Then let the children hang the matching cards from the second set on the appropriate hooks in the right-hand row.

556 | Number Pegboard

Prepare a teaching pegboard as described in prop 552. Write different numerals on one set of cards and draw corresponding numbers of dots or small pictures on another set. Hang one set of cards on the peg hooks in the left-hand row. Then let the children hang the matching cards from the second set on the appropriate hooks in the right-hand row.

557 | Shape Pegboard

Prepare a teaching pegboard as described in prop 552. Draw different geometric shapes (a circle, a square, a triangle, etc.) on one set of cards and matching geometric shapes or shape pictures (a ball, a box, a clown hat, etc.) on another set. Hang one set of cards on the peg hooks in the left-hand row. Then let the children hang the matching cards from the second set on the appropriate hooks in the right-hand row.

558 | More Teaching Pegboard Ideas

Prepare a teaching pegboard as directed in prop 552 for matching picture stickers; pictures cut from canned goods labels, magazine ads, etc.; patterned squares of wallpaper or wrapping paper; pictures of animal mothers and animal babies, animals and animal homes, etc.

559 | Basic Teaching Placemats

Make gameboards on large sheets of construction paper and cover them with clear self-stick paper. Then use the gameboards as placemats and let the children play games on them before snacktime.

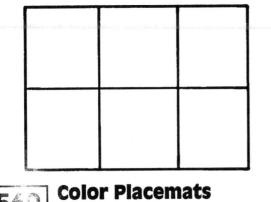

560 | Color Placemats

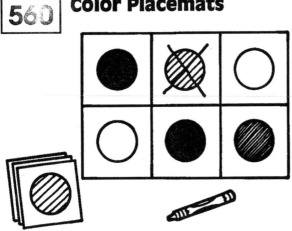

Divide large sheets of construction paper into six or more squares each and draw different colored circles in the squares. Cover with clear self-stick paper. Draw matching colored circles on index cards. As you hold up a card, have the children use crayons to X-out the matching colored circles on their gameboards. When the game is over, wipe the gameboards with a dry paper towel to remove the crayon.

561 | Number Placemats

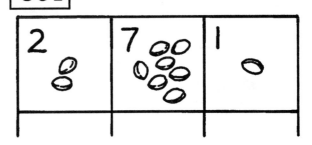

Divide large sheets of construction paper into six or more squares each and write different numerals in the upper left-hand corners of the squares. Set out a large bowl of dried beans, raisins, etc., to use as markers. Then let the children place corresponding numbers of markers in the squares on their gameboards.

562 | Picture Placemats
To make each gameboard, cover a large rectangle of wrapping paper that contains a pattern of pictures with clear self-stick paper. From a matching sheet of wrapping paper, cut out five or six of the pictures and cover them with clear self-stick paper also. Tape squares of posterboard on the backs of the gameboards to make envelopes for holding the cutouts. Then let the children match the pictures on the gameboards.

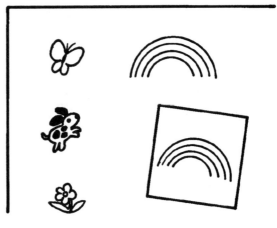

563 Shape Placemats

Make a gameboard for each group of two or three children. In the upper left-hand corner of a large piece of construction paper, draw a circle and write "Start" inside of it. Then draw a pathway of geometric shapes (circles, squares, triangles, etc.), in random order, winding around the paper. End with a circle in the lower right-hand corner marked "Finish." Make three or four game cards for each shape by drawing the shapes on index cards. Put the deck of cards face down and give each child a different kind of game marker to place on the "Start" circle. As each child turns up a card, have the child move his or her marker to the next shape designated by the card.

Teaching Pockets

564 Basic Teaching Pockets

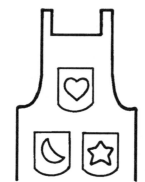

Cut four to six large pocket shapes out of different colors of felt and sew them on a butcher-style apron. Cut shapes, numerals, etc., out of felt and place them on the pockets. Then put on the apron and let the children take turns placing small objects or concept cards into the pockets as you give directions.

565 Alphabet Pockets

Make an apron as described in prop 564. Cut different upper-case letters out of felt and place them on the pockets. Write corresponding lower-case letters on posterboard squares and ask the children to put them into the appropriate pockets.

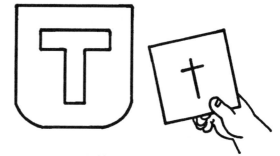

566 Beginning Sounds Pockets

Make an apron as described in prop 564. Cut different alphabet letters out of felt and place them on the pockets. Provide a collection of small objects whose names begin with those letters and ask the children to put them into the appropriate pockets.

567 Color Pockets

Make an apron as described in prop 564. Discuss the apron pocket colors and ask the children to find small matching colored objects around the room. Then have them put the objects into the appropriate pockets.

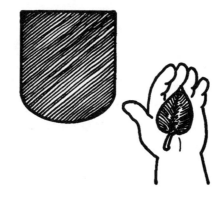

568 Number Pockets

Make an apron as described in prop 564. Cut different numerals out of felt and place them on the pockets. Then ask the children to put corresponding numbers of small objects in the pockets.

569 Shape Pockets

Make an apron as described in prop 564. Cut different basic shapes (a circle, a square, a triangle, a star, etc.) out of felt and place them on the pockets. Cut matching shapes out of posterboard and ask the children to put them into the appropriate pockets.

570 More Teaching Pocket Ideas

Use the apron described in prop 564 to sort small toys (plastic animals, cars and trucks, etc.) or pictures of foods, clothing, etc. (Make concept cards to place on the pockets by backing pictures with felt strips.)

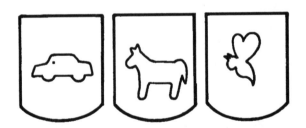

Teaching Puzzles

571 Basic Teaching Puzzles

Cut five or six index cards into two-part puzzles. Draw a shape, an alphabet letter, etc., on one part of each puzzle and a matching shape,

letter, etc., on the other part. Then mix up the puzzle pieces and let the children take turns finding the match-ups.

572 Alphabet Puzzles

Cut five or six index cards into two-part puzzles. Write a different upper-case letter on one part of each puzzle and a corresponding lower-case letter on the other part.

573 Beginning Sounds Puzzles

Cut five or six index cards into two-part puzzles. Write a different alphabet letter on one part of each puzzle and draw a picture of something whose name begins with that letter on the other part.

574 Color Puzzles

Cut five or six index cards into two-part puzzles. Draw a different colored circle on one part of each puzzle and a matching colored circle on the other part. Or write a different color word ("Red," "Blue," etc.) on one part of each puzzle and draw a matching colored circle on the other part.

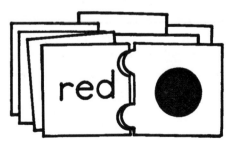

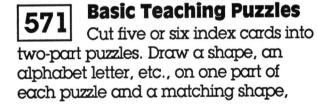

575 Shape Puzzles

Cut five or six index cards into two-part puzzles. Draw a different basic shape (a circle, a square, a triangle, a star, etc.) on one part of each puzzle and a matching shape on the other part.

576 More Teaching Puzzle Ideas

Make two-part puzzles as directed in prop 571 for matching spelling words with pictures; patterns (stripes, squiggles, etc.); pieces of textured materials (velvet, burlap, sandpaper, etc.); pictures of animals, foods, vehicles, etc.

Teaching Shapes

577 Basic Teaching Shapes

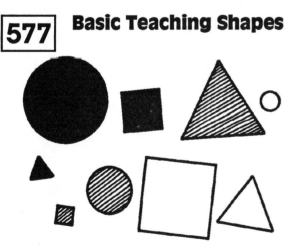

From red posterboard, cut out a large circle, a medium-sized square and a small triangle. From yellow posterboard, cut out a large square, a medium-sized triangle and a small circle. From blue posterboard, cut out a large triangle, a medium-sized circle and a small square. Mix up the shapes and lay them out on a tabletop or on the

floor. Then have the children sort the shapes as you give directions. (If desired, make more than one set of shapes out of each color of posterboard.)

578 Color Shapes

Prepare the teaching shapes as described in prop 577. Ask the children to place the red shapes in one pile, the yellow shapes in another pile and the blue shapes in a third pile. Or ask them to lay out the shapes in a pattern (yellow, blue, red, yellow, blue, red, etc.).

579 Number Shapes

Prepare the teaching shapes as described in prop 577. Ask the children to count the shapes by color, by size and by kind of shape. Or ask them to place three shapes next to two shapes, etc., and then tell how many shapes there are all together.

580 Picture Shapes

Prepare the teaching shapes as described in prop 577. Let the children put the shapes together on the tabletop or on the floor to make designs or pictures.

581 Shape Shapes

Prepare the teaching shapes as described in prop 577. Ask the children to place the circles in one pile, the squares in another pile and the triangles in a third pile. Or ask them to lay out the shapes in a pattern (triangle, square, circle, triangle, square, circle, etc.).

582 Size Shapes

Prepare the teaching shapes as described in prop 577. Ask the children to place the large shapes in one pile, the medium-sized shapes in another pile and the small shapes in a third pile. Or ask them to place each set of shapes in a pile with the largest shape on the bottom, the medium-sized shape in the middle and the smallest shape on the top.

583 More Teaching Shape Ideas

Prepare the teaching shapes as described in prop 577. Use the shapes as patterns for tracing designs on construction paper.

Teaching Snacks

584 Basic Teaching Snacks

Once or twice a week, prepare snacks to reinforce different learning concepts. Discuss the characteristics of each snack at serving time. Then let the children eat while they learn from the special snack you have prepared.

585 Color Snacks

Choose a color such as red and serve red snack items (strawberries, red gelatin, cranapple juice, red apple slices, etc.). Use red placemats and napkins, too, if desired.

586 Number Snacks

Choose a number such as "3" and serve snack items in groups of threes (three raisins, three peanuts, three banana slices, three crackers, etc.).

587 Shape Snacks

Choose a geometric shape such as a circle and serve round snack items (round crackers, cucumber slices, blueberries, O-shaped cereal, sandwiches cut into rounds, etc.).

588 | Size Snacks

Serve combinations of large and small snack items (sandwiches and raisins, orange segments and shelled peanuts, etc.).

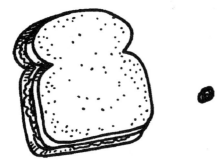

589 | Texture Snacks

Serve combinations of different textured snack items (soft banana slices and crunchy pretzels, creamy yogurt and chewy fruit leather, etc.).

590 | More Teaching Snacks

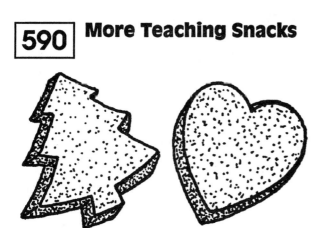

Use cookie cutters to cut sandwiches or finger Jell-O into holiday shapes, animal shapes, etc. Serve snacks that tie in with units you are teaching (fry bread for a unit on American Indians, carrot sticks dipped in honey for a unit on bees, etc.). Prepare snacks with the children to teach math and science concepts (weighing and measuring, observing how foods change as they are processed and cooked, etc.).

Teaching Stamps

591 | Basic Teaching Stamps

Carve or cut a variety of stamping materials (potato halves, sponges, gum erasers, corks, etc.) into different shapes (stars, flowers, squares, etc.). Make paint pads by placing folded paper towels in plastic foam food trays and pouring on paints. Set out the carved stamps along with cookie cutters, wooden blocks, etc. Then let the children dip the stamps into the paint and press them on their papers to make prints.

592 | Color Stamps

Choose a color such as red and prepare red paint pads. Then let the children use a variety of stamps to print red shapes on their papers.

593 | Holiday Stamps

Choose a holiday shape such as a heart and cut a variety of stamping materials (potato halves, sponges, gum erasers, corks, etc.) into heart shapes. Then let the children use the stamps, along with heart-shaped cookie cutters, to print red and pink hearts on their papers.

594 Number Stamps

At the top of each paper, write a numeral such as "3." Then let the children use a variety of stamps to print different sets of three shapes (three diamonds, three fish, etc.) on their papers.

595 Pattern Stamps

Use stamps to start patterns for the children to continue printing down the lengths of their papers (red, blue, red, blue; circle, square, triangle, circle, square, triangle; etc.).

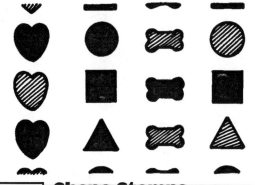

596 Shape Stamps

Choose a geometric shape, such as a circle, and cut a variety of stamping materials (potato halves, sponges, gum erasers, corks, etc.) into circle shapes. Then let the children use the stamps, along with jar lids, spools, etc., to print circle shapes on their papers.

597 More Teaching Stamp Ideas

Match color prints; match shape prints. Classify colors (red prints on one side of the paper, blue prints on the other side, etc.); classify shapes (circle prints on one side of the paper, square prints on the other side, etc.).

Teaching Sticks

598 Basic Teaching Sticks

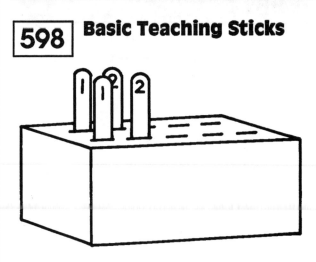

Turn a shoebox upside down and cut two parallel rows of slits in the top. Decorate the ends of one set of tongue depressors with shape stickers, alphabet letters, etc. Decorate the ends of another set of tongue depressors to match. Insert one set of tongue depressors in one of the rows of slits. Then let the children insert matching tongue depressors from the second set in the appropriate slits in the other row.

599 Alphabet Sticks

Prepare a teaching sticks game as directed in prop 598, writing different upper-case letters on one set of tongue depressors and corresponding lower-case letters on another set.

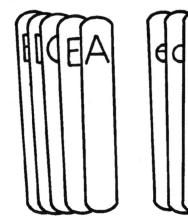

600 Color Sticks

Prepare a teaching sticks game as directed in prop 598, attaching different colored stickers to one set of tongue depressors and matching colored stickers to another set.

601 Number Sticks

Prepare a teaching sticks game as directed in prop 598, writing different numerals on one set of tongue depressors and attaching corresponding numbers of stickers to another set.

602 Picture Sticks

Prepare a teaching sticks game as directed in prop 598, attaching different picture stickers to one set of tongue depressors and matching picture stickers to another set.

603 Shape Sticks

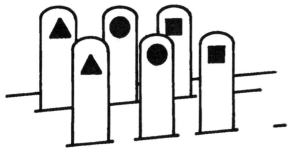

Prepare a teaching sticks game as directed in prop 598, attaching stickers cut into different basic shapes (a circle, a square, a triangle, a star, etc.) to one set of tongue depressors and matching shaped stickers to another set.

604 More Teaching Sticks Ideas

Make sticks for sorting colors (red in one row, blue in the other row, etc.); make sticks for sorting shapes (circles in one row, squares in the other row, etc.). Use unmarked tongue depressors for playing counting games.

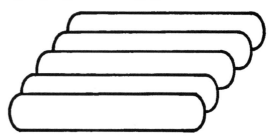

Teaching Wheel

605 Basic Teaching Wheel

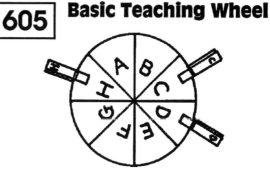

Cut a 12-inch circle out of posterboard. Divide the circle into eight sections and draw shapes, alphabet letters, etc., in the sections. Draw matching shapes, letters, etc., on eight clothespins. Then let the children clip the clothespins around the edge of the wheel on the matching sections.

606 Alphabet Wheel

Prepare a teaching wheel as described in prop 605, writing a different upper-case letter in each section of the wheel. Write corresponding lower-case letters on eight clothespins.

607 Beginning Sounds Wheel

Prepare a teaching wheel as described in prop 605, drawing a picture of something whose name begins with a different sound in each section of the wheel (a balloon in one section, a leaf in another section, etc.). Write the corresponding beginning alphabet letters on eight clothespins.

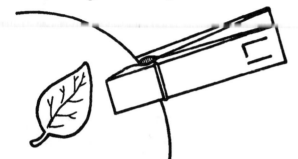

608 Color Wheel

Prepare a teaching wheel as described in prop 605, coloring each section of the wheel a different color. Color eight clothespins to match.

609 Number Wheel

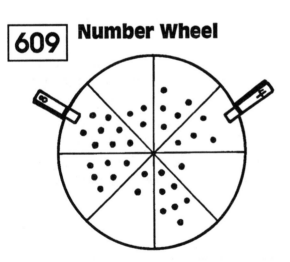

Prepare a teaching wheel as described in prop 605, drawing a different number of dots or small pictures in each section of the wheel. Write corresponding numerals on eight clothespins.

610 Shape Wheel

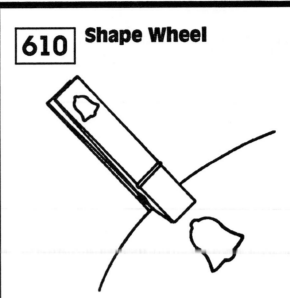

Prepare a teaching wheel as described in prop 605, drawing a different basic shape (a circle, a square, a triangle, a star, etc.) in each section of the wheel. Draw matching shapes on eight clothespins.

611 More Teaching Wheel Ideas

Prepare a teaching wheel as described in prop 605 for matching pieces of textured materials (velvet, burlap, sandpaper, etc.); pieces of patterned wallpaper or wrapping paper; etc.

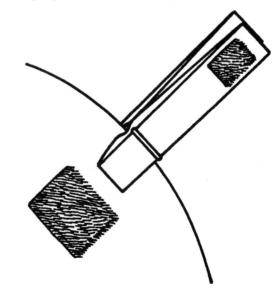

Teaching Windows

612 | Basic Teaching Windows

Tape a row of clear plastic photo holders down each side of a large sheet of posterboard. Attach a brass paper fastener next to each photo holder toward the center of the board. Cut index cards to fit inside of the photo holders. Draw pictures, shapes, etc., on one set of cards and insert them in the photo holders in the left-hand row. Make a matching set of cards and insert them in the photo holders in the right-hand row in a different order. Tie short pieces of yarn to the paper fasteners on the left. Then let the children match the cards by winding the loose ends of the yarn pieces around the appropriate paper fasteners on the right. Change the cards in the photo holders each day to reinforce a different learning concept.

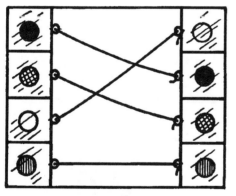

613 | Animal Windows

Prepare teaching windows as described in prop 612. Put cards containing pictures of different animal mothers in the photo holders on the left. Put cards containing pictures of corresponding animal babies or animal homes in the photo holders on the right.

614 | Beginning Sounds Windows

Prepare teaching windows as described in prop 612. Put cards containing different alphabet letters in the photo holders on the left. Put cards containing pictures of things whose names begin with those letters in the photo holders on the right.

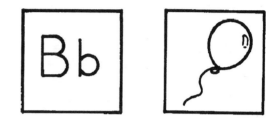

615 | Color Windows

Prepare teaching windows as described in prop 612. Put different colored cards in the photo holders on the left. Put matching colored cards or cards containing matching colored pictures in the photo holders on the right.

616 | Number Windows

Prepare teaching windows as described in prop 612. Put cards containing different numerals in the photo holders on the left. Put cards containing corresponding numbers of dots or small pictures in the photo holders on the right.

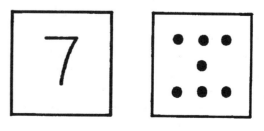

617 Shape Windows

Prepare teaching windows as described in prop 612. Put cards containing different geometric shapes (a circle, a square, a triangle, etc.) in the photo holders on the left. Put cards containing matching geometric shapes or shape pictures (a ball, a clown hat, etc.) in the photo holders on the right.

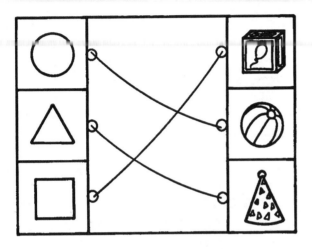

618 More Teaching Windows Ideas

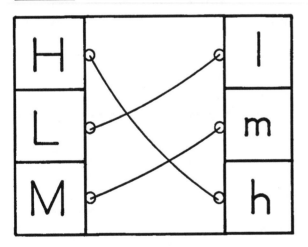

Prepare teaching windows as described in prop 612 for matching upper-case letters with lower-case letters; squares of patterned wallpaper or wrapping paper; pictures of holiday shapes, foods, articles of clothing, etc.

Teaching Worm

619 Basic Teaching Worm

Cut a large, rounded worm shape out of construction paper. Use a felt-tip marker to draw on facial features and to divide the worm into six or more sections. On opposite sides of each dividing line, draw matching shapes, patterns, etc. Cover the worm shape with clear self-stick paper and cut out the sections. Then let the children piece the worm together by matching the shapes, patterns, etc., on the ends of the sections.

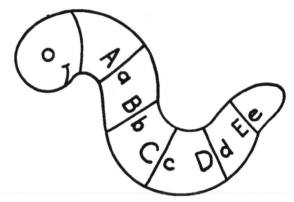

620 Color Worm

Prepare a teaching worm as directed in prop 619, coloring the area on one side of each dividing line a different color and the other side a matching color.

621 Number Worm

Prepare a teaching worm as directed in 619, writing a different numeral on one side of each dividing line and draw a corresponding number of dots or small pictures on the other side.

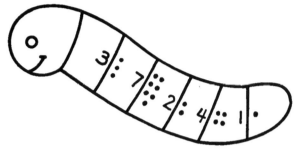

622 Pattern Worm

Prepare a teaching worm as directed in prop 619, drawing a different pattern (stripes, squiggles, etc.) in the area on one side of each dividing line and a matching pattern in the area on the other side.

623 Shape Worm

Prepare a teaching worm as directed in prop 619, drawing a different basic shape (a circle, a square, a triangle, a star, etc.) on one side of each dividing line and a matching shape on the other side.

624 Texture Worm

Prepare a teaching worm as directed in prop 619, gluing a piece of different textured material on one half of each dividing line and a piece of matching textured material on the other side. (Cover just the back of the worm shape with clear self-stick paper.)

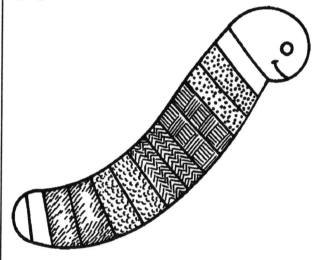

625 More Teaching Worm Ideas

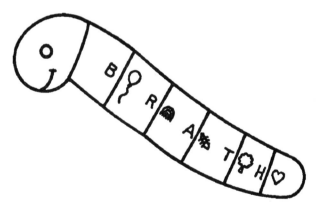

Prepare a teaching worm as directed in prop 619, for matching upper-case letters with lower-case letters; alphabet letters with pictures of things whose names begin with those letters; picture stickers.

Outdoor Props

Bubble Blowers

626 | Basic Bubble Recipe I

Mix together ¼ cup Joy dishwashing detergent, ½ cup water, a few drops of food coloring and 1 teaspoon sugar. Pour into a shallow container. Let the bubble solution age for a few days for the best results.

627 | Basic Bubble Recipe II

Mix together 2 cups Joy dishwashing detergent, 6 cups water and ¾ cup Karo light corn syrup. Shake and let sit for a few hours. (Note: This solution makes blowing bubbles easy for even very young children, but it also make the ground where the bubbles pop very slippery.)

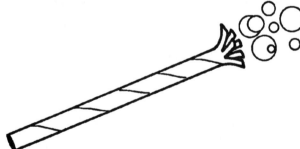

628 | Bent Straw Bubble Blower

Make 1-inch slits around one end of a plastic drinking straw. Bend the strips back. Dip that end of the straw into a bubble solution and blow through the other end.

629 | Coat Hanger Bubble Wand

Untwist a wire coat hanger. Wrap the hanger around a coffee can or other circular object to make the circular part of the bubble wand. Twist the wires in place. Leave 4 inches of straight wire for a handle and use wire cutters to snip off the rest of the hanger.

630 | Double Bubble Blower

Cut four ½-inch slits in each end of a plastic drinking straw. Curl the cut strips backward. Then make a cut ¾ of the way through the middle of the straw. Bend the straw in half at the cut. Dip the two ends into a bubble solution and blow into the cut in the middle of the straw to make two bubbles at the same time.

631 Egg Carton Bubble Blower

Cut an egg cup out of a plastic foam egg carton and poke a ¼-inch hole in the bottom of it. Dip the rim of the egg cup into a bubble solution and blow through the hole.

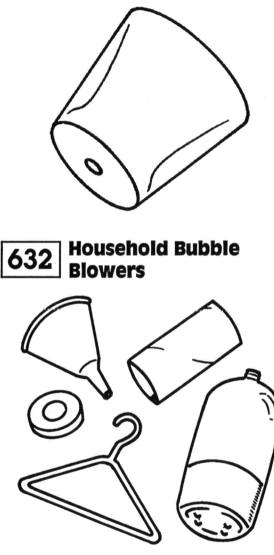

632 Household Bubble Blowers

You can make bubble blowers from common household items such as these: a funnel, a juice can with both ends removed, a plastic hanger, a clear-plastic 2-liter bottle with the tips of the bumps on the bottom cut off, a plastic lid with the center removed.

633 Multiple Bubble Blower

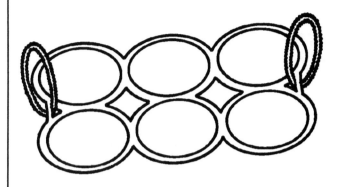

Fasten pipe cleaner handles onto the sides of a plastic six-pack holder and dip it into a bubble solution. Blow through all six holes at once to make multiple bubbles.

634 Paper Cup Bubble Blower

Cut out the bottom of a paper cup. Dip the top rim of the cup into a bubble solution and blow through the bottom hole.

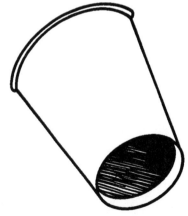

635 Single Bubble Blower

Cut one ring off of a plastic six-pack holder. Fasten pipe cleaner handles to the sides of the ring. Dip the ring into a bubble solution and blow.

636 Straw Bundle Bubble Blower

Tape four to six straws together. Dip one end of the bundle into a bubble solution and blow through the other end.

637 Super Bubble Blower

Thread 3 feet of string through two drinking straws and tie the ends of the string together. Pour a bubble solution that contains more detergent than water into a large pan or tray. Wet your fingers and, holding the sides of the straws together, dip the bubble maker into the solution for 20 to 30 seconds. Remove the bubble maker from the solution and pull the straws apart until you have a bubble "screen." Gently wave the bubble screen through the air, then bring the straws together to make a bubble.

638 Campfire

Create a portable "campfire" by nailing or gluing three or four logs together. Insert strips of red foil or construction paper between the logs to resemble flames.

639 Camping Equipment

Collect camping equipment to let the children use while they are pretending to camp out. Suggested equipment includes: army surplus mess kits, flashlights, sleeping bags, camp stools, compasses and lanterns.

640 Fishing Poles

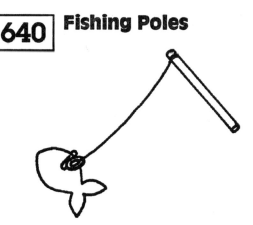

Attach string or yarn to the ends of small wooden sticks or dowels. Tie a circular magnet to each string. Let the children "fish" for construction paper fish shapes that have paper clips attached to them.

641 Tent

Set up a tent outdoors. If you do not have access to a commercial tent, make one by draping a blanket over a clothesline or some chairs.

Gardening Props

642 Individual Tire Planters

For each child fill the center of an old tire with dirt or potting soil. Let the children each choose one or two plants to grow in his or her planter.

643 Stakes

Purchase stakes to use in a children's garden for labeling various areas and for supporting tall plants.

644 String Bean Tepee

Use long wooden stakes or poles to make a string bean tepee by pushing the stakes into the dirt in a circle. Tie the top ends of the stakes together. Guide the bean plants up the poles as they grow. Be sure to leave an opening for a door.

645 Tire Garden

Old tires can be used as miniature gardens for the children. Fill the centers of the tires with dirt or potting soil. Have the children work together to plant different kinds of seeds in each tire.

646 Wagons

Have the children use wagons as they plant, weed or harvest their gardens.

647 Watering Cans
Fill small watering cans with water. Let the children take turns watering plants as needed.

648 Wheelbarrow Planter
Use a wheelbarrow as a planter. Fill it halfway with dirt and plant some seeds. Let the children move the wheelbarrow to keep it in the sun throughout the day.

Motor Development Props

649 Bean Bag Toss
Lay a Hula-Hoop on the ground and have the children try tossing bean bags inside of it.

650 Character Target
Paint a favorite character or shape on a large piece of wood. Attach the target to a fence or other support outdoors. Let the children toss balls, snowballs or beanbags at the target.

651 Circle Target

Paint a traditional circular target on a large piece of wood. Attach the target to a fence or other support outdoors. Let the children use the target as a goal for a ball, a snowball, a beanbag or squirted water.

652 Concrete Pipe
Set a concrete drainage pipe in the play yard so that it will not roll around. Pack dirt or sand around it so the children can climb on top of it. Let the children crawl over, through or on top of the pipe.

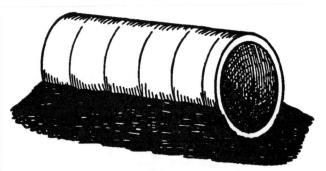

653 Hoop Ball Toss
Hang a Hula-Hoop from a tree and let the children take turns tossing balls through it.

654 Hoop Jumping
Lay Hula-Hoops on the ground in a path and let the children take turns jumping in and out of them.

Hoop Roll
Let the children roll Hula Hoops back and forth to one another.

 Hoop Spin
Have the children hold onto the outside of a Hula-Hoop and try to spin around together.

657 **Kick Ball Holder**

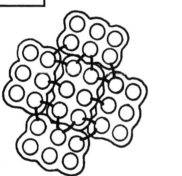 

Collect several plastic holders from aluminum can six-packs. Tie enough holders together to surround a large, lightweight ball. Place the ball inside the holder and hang it a few inches above the ground with a sturdy rope. Let the children take turns kicking the ball.

658 **Kicking Net**
Attach a lightweight rope net to two poles and let the children kick balls into it.

 Parachute
Locate an old parachute. Place yarn balls or other light objects in the center of the parachute. Have the children hold onto the edges of the parachute and move it up and down to make the balls "dance."

 Rope Net
Secure a sturdy rope net to a vertical platform and let the children use it for climbing.

 Waist Spin
Have older children spin Hula-Hoops around their waists and see who can keep the hoops spinning the longest.

Riding Props

662 **Car Wash**
Cut off both ends of a large cardboard appliance box. Reinforce the box by wrapping tape around its sides. In the center of the box hang a row of fabric strips across the top of the box. Have the children ride their tricycles through the "car wash."

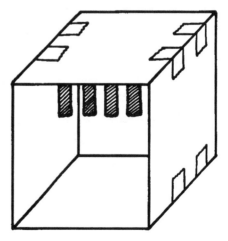

663 Cardboard Box Vehicle

Cut the top and bottom off a cardboard box. Decorate the box to resemble a police car, a fire engine or other emergency vehicle. Attach two ribbon straps to the box that go from the front to the back. Help a child step into the box and place the straps over his or her shoulders. Then have the child "drive" his or her emergency vehicle through the tricycle play area.

664 Fire Hose

Set out a garden hose with a pistol-grip nozzle. Let the children pretend they are firefighters. Have them coil the hose neatly in a wagon. Then have them quickly pull out the wagon and hose whenever there is a "fire."

665 Gas Pump

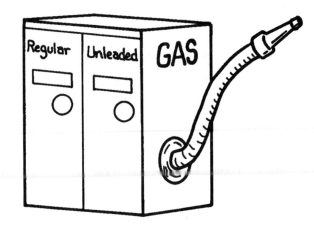

Cut a small hole in the side of a medium-sized cardboard box. Cut off three or four feet from the end of an old garden hose. Insert the cut end of the hose into the hole in the box and securely tape it in place. Attach a pistol-grip nozzle to the other end of the hose. Add details to the box with felt-tip markers as desired.

666 Licenses

Make a pretend driver's license for each child. Thread the licenses on loops of yarn for the children to wear while they are riding tricycles. They will be more likely to follow the safety rules if they know that their licenses will be suspended for "reckless driving."

667 Parade Prop Box

Keep a box filled with the following parade props: crepe paper streamers, large feathers, balloons, ribbons, stickers and masking tape. Let the children decorate tricycles and wagons and ride along a designated parade route.

668 Permanent Roads And Parking Spaces

If you have a concrete tricycle riding area, you can create permanent parking spaces and roads by painting white or yellow stripes on the concrete.

669 Temporary Roads And Parking Spaces

Make temporary stripes for roads and parking spaces in your tricycle riding area with chalk or masking tape.

670 Tow Truck

Tie a 6-foot length of rope to the back of a tricycle. Let a child tie the loose end of the rope to another tricycle, a wagon or a box and tow it.

671 Traffic Signs

Cut plywood into geometric shapes and paint them to resemble real street signs. Nail wooden stakes to the signs and stand them in cans filled with cement or dirt. Place the signs around your riding area and encourage the children to follow them. To keep the children on their toes, periodically move the signs around.

672 Wagon Panels

Cut two long narrow rectangles out of cardboard. Decorate the rectangles to look like the sides of a bakery truck, a fire engine or other vehicle. Attach the rectangles to the sides of a wagon. Let the children use the paneled wagon in your tricycle play area.

Sandboxes

673 Infant Bathtub

Fill a plastic infant bathtub with sand to make a portable sandbox. The sand can be used wet or dry. Store the tub indoors when not in use.

674 Tire Sandboxes

Cut an old tire in half to make two rounds. Lay both rounds on the ground and fill them with sand to make small sandboxes.

675 Wading Pools
Set several small inflatable wading pools in different places around the yard. Fill the wading pools with sand for the children to play in.

Snow Props

676 Bathtub Sled
Use a plastic infant bathtub for a sled. Its sides will keep a small child from falling out, and it will not go too fast. Punch a hole in the rim and attach a rope, if desired.

677 Cardboard Sled
Cut a large rectangle out of a sturdy piece of cardboard. Let a child use the cardboard rectangle like a sled.

678 Dishpan Sled
Use a dishpan for a sled. Attach a rope to the rim of the tub for a handle, if desired.

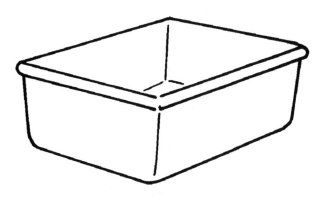

679 Inner Tube Sled
Find an old inner tube and fill it with air. Use the inner tube sled on a gently sloping hill.

680 Kitchen Molds
Use gelatin molds and plastic containers for winter fun. Let the children pack them with snow to make three-dimensional shapes.

681 Plastic Tray Sleds
Collect plastic trays. Let the children use them for sledding.

682 Spray Bottles
Fill spray bottles with water and add food coloring. Let the children spray the colored water on snow to make designs.

Swings

683 Board Swing

Cut an 8- by 14-inch rectangle out of ¾-inch wood. Drill a hole in each corner. Thread a sturdy rope through a hole in one side of the board and up through the other hole. Tie the end of the rope to the rest of the rope 6 inches above the holes. Repeat for the other side of the board. Tie the ends of the ropes securely to a sturdy tree branch and adjust the ropes to make the seat hang evenly.

684 Box Swing

Purchase a sturdy plastic milk box. Cut off the front of the box and sand any rough edges. Tie sturdy ropes securely to the box by looping them through holes in the sides. Tie the ends of the ropes to a strong tree limb.

685 Tire Swing

Tie a sturdy rope to an old tire. Hang the tire from a strong tree branch.

686 Toy Swing

Attach yarn or ribbon to the arms or around the middle of a stuffed animal. Tie the yarn to a tree branch. Let the children take turns pushing the stuffed animal back and forth.

687 Batting Stand

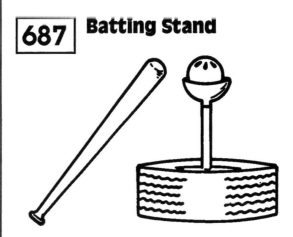

Fill the center an old tire with cement. Place the handle of a plunger in the cement. Let the children take turns placing a ball in the upside-down plunger and hitting it with a bat.

688 Net Poles

Fill the centers of two old tires with cement. Stand a wooden or metal pole in each cement-filled tire. Use the poles to hold up game nets.

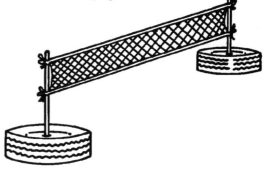

689 Tether Ball Pole

Use one of the net poles from prop 688 to hang up a tether ball.

690 Tire Walk

Place a number of tires flat on the ground. Let the children walk across or run around them.

691 Upright Tires

Place tires in cement in an upright position so that the top halves of the tires are above the cement. Let the children sit or bounce on the tires.

Water Props

692 Car Wash

Help the children set up a neighborhood car wash on the sidewalk or in a driveway. Hook up a garden hose and get out a few buckets and sponges. Let the children help you wash your car or have them invite their friends over to wash their tricycles.

693 Handy Squirter

Use a straight pin to poke a hole at the tip of each finger of a rubber glove. Fill the glove with water. Let the children squeeze the fingers to make the water squirt out.

694 Paintbrushes

Give the children buckets of water and large, clean paintbrushes. Let them pretend that they are house painters and have them "paint" the sides of a house with water.

695 Rain Gutter

Buy a 10-foot section of plastic rain gutter (available at home and garden stores). Raise one end of the gutter and let it slope gently into a tub of water. Let the children take turns sliding objects down the gutter into the water.

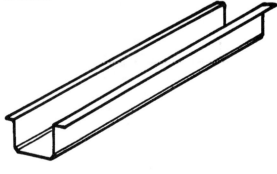

696 Shower Bucket

Make a simple outdoor shower by punching holes in the bottom of an old bucket and hanging it from a hook or a tree limb. Run a garden hose from a water spigot to the bucket, tying the hose in place as needed. Turn on the water and let the children run and play under the outdoor shower.

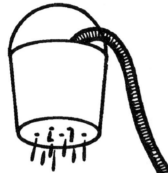

697 Siphon

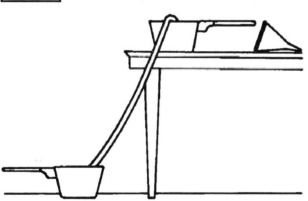

Set out 5 feet of ½-inch plastic tubing, a plug for one end of the tube and a plastic funnel. Place a pan of water on an outdoor table and an empty pan on the ground. Plug one end of the tube. Place a funnel in the other end and have the children fill the tube with water by pouring water into the funnel. Remove the funnel and place the open end of the tube into the pan of

water. Then help the children place the plugged end of the tube into the empty pan and remove the plug. The water will be siphoned from the top pan down into the one on the ground.

698 Tire Moats

Cut an old tire in half to make rounds. Lay both rounds on the ground and fill them with water to create moats for pretend castles or circular rivers for sailing toy boats.

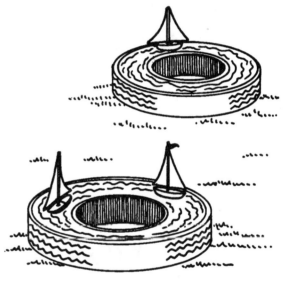

699 Wading Pools

Set several small wading pools in various areas around the yard. Fill the pools with water for the children to play in.

700 Water Slide

Place a 3- by 8-foot piece of vinyl on a grassy slope. Secure a garden hose at the top of the vinyl so that the water will run down it, keeping it wet. Let the children take turns sliding down the vinyl. Supervision is recommended with this activity to insure that only one child at a time takes a turn.

More Outdoor Props

701 | Bleach Bottle Megaphones

Cut off the top halves of several bleach bottles that have handles and wash them very carefully. Let the children use them outdoors for megaphones.

702 | Bush Hideout

If you have a large bush or hedge in the play yard, consider cutting out a crawl space or a quiet hide-away space for the children.

703 | Cable Spool Tables

Collect empty wooden cable spools from electricians, hardware stores, etc. and use them as outdoor project tables. Place them in the middle of a sandbox for stand-up sand play. Or use the spools as outdoor snack, playdough, art project or mud pie tables.

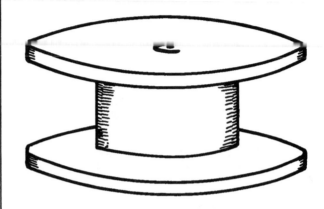

704 | Clothesline

String a clothesline between two trees, chairs or other sturdy objects. Set out a basketful of small clothes and spring-type clothespins. Let the children take turns hanging up the clothes.

705 | Soapy Water

Set a plastic dishpan filled with warm soapy water next to a clothesline and let the children wash clothes before hanging them up.

Prop Boxes

706 | Creating the Boxes

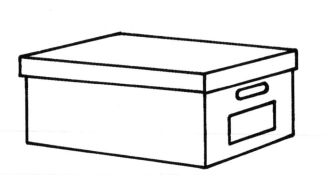

Obtain large storage boxes with sturdy lids. Label each box with a different occupation or theme. Ask family and friends to help fill the boxes with appropriate play items. Store the boxes and bring out only one per day. Suggestions for a variety of boxes and their contents follow.

707 | Bakery Box

Playdough, rolling pins, garlic press, birthday candles, small round pans, small loaf pans, muffin tins, cookie sheets, cake decoration items, chef hats, aprons, bake shop sign, price signs on toothpicks, dull knives, cookie cutters, hot pads or oven mitts, cooling racks.

708 | Bank Box

Play money, money sorting box, note pads, deposit slips, pens, pencils, bank sign, green visors, purses, wallets, metal box for a safe, locks with keys.

709 | Beach Box

Sunglasses, beach towels, buckets, small shovels, beach balls, air mattresses, diving masks, snorkels, fins, beach umbrella, empty suntan lotion bottles, sun hats, visors, portable radio, travel posters of beach areas.

710 | Camping Box

Tent or blankets and rope for making one, flashlights, logs for a campfire, sleeping bags, compasses, mess kits, picnic basket, cooking utensils, pans, small backpacks, battery-operated lanterns.

711 Circus Box

Crepe paper streamers for decorating circus parade vehicles and making the outline of a large circus tent, top hat for the ring master, long pieces of thick yarn for making circus rings and balance beams, tutus, clown hats, clown noses, Hula-Hoops, stuffed animals, large balls.

712 Construction Box

Rulers, tape measures, hard hats, blueprints, small hammers, small saws, levels, tool aprons, scraps of wood, large-headed nails, sawhorses.

713 Fix-It Box

Screwdrivers, large screws, softwood, plastic foam pieces, tape measures, tool aprons, locks, hinges, nuts, bolts, knobs, broken toys, old radios, masking tape.

714 Florist Box

Plastic or silk flowers, green stem wrap, plastic vases, gift cards, tissue paper, small baskets, pieces of plastic foam or playdough.

715 Garden Box

Watering cans, small shovels, trowels, rakes, garden gloves, empty seed packets, knee pads, wooden stakes, small section of fencing.

716 Grocery Store Box

Plastic fruits and vegetables; empty food containers (cereal and dry goods boxes, milk cartons, egg cartons, food cans, TV dinner boxes, etc.), grocery bags, baskets, bins, cash register, play money, plastic foam meat trays with pictures of meat glued on them and covered with plastic wrap, box of coupons, purses, grocery store sign, newspaper grocery ads to hang on the wall.

717 Hawaii Box

Grass skirts, plastic flower leis, grass mats, Hawaiian shirts, sun hats, visors, sunglasses, small muumuus, silk flowers to pin in hair, prisms for making rainbows, Hawaiian travel posters, books about Hawaii, plastic pineapples.

718 Hospital Box

Adhesive bandages, tongue depressors, cotton balls, stethoscopes, gauze, face masks, white jackets, small bottles, hospital sign, doctor's bag or a shaving kit labeled with a red vinyl tape cross.

719 House Cleaning Box

Brooms, dustpans, rags, dust mops, buckets, sponges, mops, spray bottles, scrub brushes, polishing cloths, dish-pans, small hand-held vacuum.

720 Jewelry Store Box

Fake jewelry (necklaces, clip-on ear-rings, rings, old watches, etc.), magni-fying glasses, small jewelry gift boxes with cotton squares, cardboard cutouts of hands to display rings, jewelry store sign, small sacks, price tags, cash register.

721 Magic Box

Black capes, black top hats, magic wands, magic props (toy bunny, plastic chicken, etc.), simple magic tricks (disappearing penny container, magic milk pitcher, etc.), silk scarves, small fold-out table, boxes, magic show sign.

722 Office Box

Paper clips, paper, clipboards, pens, pencils, envelopes, stamp-type stickers, scissors, crayons, rubber stamps, stamp pads, typewriter, telephone, note pads.

723 Painting Box

Paint buckets, paint rollers, large and small paintbrushes, paint clothes, step stool, paint edgers, paint hats, wooden paint stirrers, masking tape.

724 Restaurant Box

Tablecloths, napkins, menus, flower vases and plastic flowers, silverware, plastic plates, plastic glasses, trays, water pitchers.

725 Sewing Box

Crochet hooks, plastic yarn needles, yarn, burlap squares, drinking straws cut into sections for lacing, lacing cards, scissors, vinyl scraps punched with lacing holes for making purses and belts.

Puppets

726 Large Box Puppet

Cut the lid off of an empty detergent box, cracker box or cereal box and turn it upside down. Cut holes in the narrow sides of the box and insert cardboard toilet tissue tubes for arms. Cover the box with plain colored paper. Cut facial features out of construction paper and glue them to the front of the box. Put your hand inside the box to work the puppet.

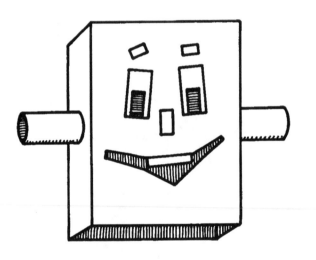

727 Milk Carton Puppet

Thoroughly wash and dry an empty half-gallon cardboard milk carton. On the back of the carton, poke a hole through the top. Insert a piece of yarn through the hole and knot the end on the inside of the carton. Then tape the top closed and cover the entire carton with construction paper, letting the yarn hang free. Approximately one-third of the way down, cut through three sides of the carton with a craft knife. Use felt-tip markers to draw eyes and a nose on the top half of the carton and a mouth around the cut. Add pieces of yarn for hair. Open and close the puppet's mouth by pulling on the yarn at the back of the carton.

728 Surprise Puppet

Cut a finger-sized hole in the bottom of a small cardboard box. Draw facial features on the palm side of your pointer fingertip. Slip your decorated finger up through the hole in the box to use the puppet. You can decorate the box so that your finger becomes a worm peeping out of its hole, a flower growing out of some grass or a jack-in-the-box.

729 Clothespin Big Mouth Puppet

Cut a circle out of an index card. Cut the circle in half, making the top half slightly larger than the bottom half. Glue the top half of the circle to the top side of a spring-type clothespin and the bottom half to the bottom side. Draw an eye on the top half with a black felt-tip marker. Squeeze the clothespin to make the puppet's mouth open and close.

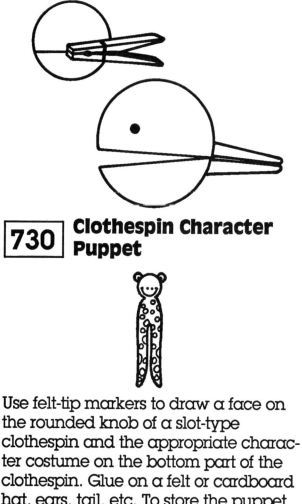

730 Clothespin Character Puppet

Use felt-tip markers to draw a face on the rounded knob of a slot-type clothespin and the appropriate character costume on the bottom part of the clothespin. Glue on a felt or cardboard hat, ears, tail, etc. To store the puppet, slip the clothespin over the rim of an empty coffee can or other similar container.

731 Caterpillar Puppet

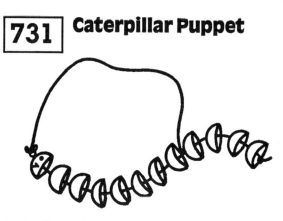

Cut all of the egg cups out of an egg carton. Poke a hole in the bottom of each cup and string the cups on a piece of yarn to make a "caterpillar." Tie knots in both ends of the yarn. Cut another piece of yarn and tie one end to the knot at the front of the caterpillar and the other end to the yarn near the eighth egg cup. Make the caterpillar crawl by holding onto the loop of yarn and moving it up and down.

732 Egg Carton Finger Creature

From a cardboard egg carton cut out, in one piece, an egg cup and two adjacent cones. Trim the cones to look like ears. Hold the egg cup so that the ears are on top and carefully cut an X-shape in the bottom side of the cup for a finger opening. Paint the puppet a desired color and add facial features with felt-tip markers.

733 Toothy Puppet

Cut the lids off two egg cartons. Cut jagged teeth around three edges of each lid, leaving one short edge uncut. Put the lids together, with the teeth facing inward, and tape the uncut ends together. Cut two 1- by 6-inch strips out of construction paper and tape one near the back of the top lid and the other one near the back of the bottom lid to make handles. Glue eyes, ears, fins, a tail, etc. in the appropriate places.

Fast Food Holder Puppets

734 French Fry Holder Pop-Up Puppet

Insert a straw into a plastic foam ball. Pull the straw out, drop some glue into the hole, then replace the straw. Allow the glue to dry. Use felt-tip markers to draw facial features on the ball. Glue short pieces of yarn to the ball for hair. Poke a hole in the bottom of a large cardboard French fry holder. With the holder upright, stick the straw down into the holder and out the hole in the bottom. Move the straw up and down to make the puppet appear and disappear.

735 Hamburger Holder Puppet

Cut the fastener tabs off of a cardboard fast food hamburger holder. Glue two plastic moving eyes on the front of the holder and add a mouth with a black felt-tip marker. Carefully poke a hole in the back of the lid and another hole near the back in the bottom of the holder. To use the puppet, put your index finger through the hole in the lid and your thumb through the hole in the bottom. Then move your finger and thumb to open and close the puppet's mouth.

736 Marching Band Puppet

Carefully open up a large cardboard French fry holder. Draw a face in the middle of the inside of it. Add other features as desired. Fold back the sides of the holder to make shoulders. Cut two horizontal slits in the holder as shown. Then weave a straw through the slits to make a handle.

737 | Finger Face Puppets

Use felt-tip markers to draw two eyes, a nose and a mouth on each finger of one hand. Use the finger face puppets to tell a multi-character story.

738 | Finger Fold-Up Puppet

Cut out a 5- by 7-inch rectangle out of paper. Fold the rectangle in half lengthwise and then in half again to make a long narrow strip. Curl the top half of the paper down and attach it to the middle of the strip with a paperclip. Draw a face on the loop and tie some yarn on the top for hair. Place a finger in the bottom end of the folded paper to work the puppet.

739 | Fingertip Puppets

Cut the fingertips off of an old glove. Use felt-tip markers to add facial features to the fingertips. Glue yarn on the tops of the fingertips for hair. Put one puppet on each finger of one hand.

740 | Nose Puppet

Turn a paper cup upside down. Cut a small circle out of the side of the cup to make a nose hole. Add eyes and a mouth with felt-tip markers. Glue pieces of yarn on top of the cup for hair. Stick a finger into the cup and out the hole to make a nose. If you wish to hide your hand, stick your finger up through the middle of a paper napkin before poking it through the paper cup.

741 | Paper Cup Puppet

Make a hole large enough for a finger in the side of a paper cup. Lay the cup on its side with the hole on the bottom. Make a nose by cutting a large circle from construction paper and gluing it on what was the bottom of the cup. Glue construction paper features to the cup in the appropriate places.

742 Paper Spider Puppet

Cut a 2-inch square out of black construction paper. Wrap the square snugly around the tip of a finger and tape it securely near the top. Cut slits around the bottom of the puppet to make legs. Fold the legs out.

743 Plastic Foam Ball Puppet

Cut two hat shapes out of felt. Glue the tops and sides of the shapes together. Then glue the hat to the top of a plastic foam ball. Add small decorations cut out of felt to the hat, if desired. Cut eye, nose and mouth shapes out of felt scraps and glue them to the plastic foam ball. Fluff out a cotton ball to use as a beard or a collar and glue in the appropriate area. Poke a hole in the bottom of the plastic foam ball with a pencil. Remove the pencil and place the puppet on a finger.

744 Polka Dot Puppets

Attach a self-stick dot to each finger of one hand. Draw facial features on each dot with a felt-tip marker.

745 Rubber Glove Puppet

Wash and dry an old rubber glove. Add facial features to each finger with a felt-tip marker. Use the glove puppet to tell a multi-character story.

746 Walking Puppet

Cut a character shape out of posterboard. Cut two finger holes about ½ inch above the bottom edge of the puppet. Use felt-tip markers to decorate the puppet as desired. Insert two fingers into the holes to make the puppet "walk."

747 Basic Hand Puppet

Cut two mitt shapes out of felt or fabric. Put the mitt shapes together and sew around the edges, leaving the bottom edge open. Decorate as desired with felt scraps, fabric scraps, buttons, felt-tip markers and yarn.

748 Felt Triangle Puppet

Cut two large triangles out of felt. Sew the triangles together along two sides, leaving a 2-inch finger hole in the middle of each side. Cut a strip out of a contrasting color of felt for the puppet's face. Add facial features cut from felt.

749 Washcloth Puppet

Cut a washcloth in half. Draw a child-sized mitt shape on each half of the washcloth. Cut the shapes out. Sew the mitt shapes together then turn them seam side in. Sew on washable items such as buttons or terrycloth shapes to make a face.

750 Big Mouth Puppet

Fold a paper plate in half. Cut two 1-by 6-inch strips out of construction paper. Glue one paper strip to the top half of the paper plate and the other paper strip to the bottom of the paper plate to make handles. Glue two cotton balls to the top half of the plate for eyes. Attach a small circle of black construction paper to each cotton ball. Cut a tongue shape out of red construction paper and glue it to the inside of the plate.

751 Hand-Held Paper Plate Puppet

Cut a paper plate in half. Position one half over the top of a whole paper plate with the fronts of the plates facing. Staple the plates together. Use construction paper and felt-tip markers to create facial features. Put your hand in the pocket on the back of the puppet to make it move.

752 Two-Faced Puppet

Tape a tongue depressor handle to the front of a paper plate. Place another paper plate over the first one, fronts facing, and staple the plates together. Glue pieces of yarn for hair on top of both plates so that it hangs down on both sides. Then use felt-tip markers to decorate each side of the puppet with a different face.

Pop-Up Puppets

753 Paper Cup Pop-Up Puppet

Insert a straw into a plastic foam ball. Pull the straw out, drop some glue into the hole, then replace the straw. Allow the glue to dry. Use felt-tip markers to draw facial features on the ball. Glue short pieces of yarn to the ball for hair. Poke a hole in the bottom of a paper drinking cup. While holding the cup upright, stick the straw down into the cup and out the hole in the bottom. Move the straw up and down to make the puppet appear and disappear.

754 Peek-A-Boo Puppet

Poke one end of a straw into a 1-inch plastic foam ball to make a hole. Remove the straw and fill the hole with glue. Put the end of the straw back into the ball and allow the glue to dry. Decorate the ball as desired to make a puppet. Put the straw down through a cardboard toilet tissue tube. Move the straw up and down to play peek-a-boo with the puppet.

755 Story Puppets

Cut two straw-sized holes in the bottom of a paper cup. Cut out two pictures of characters and one picture of scenery from a magazine or a greeting card. Tape each character picture to the end of a drinking straw. Slip the ends of the straws through the holes in the bottom of the cup. Attach the scenery picture to one side of the cup so that it stands above the rim. Let a child tell a story by moving the straws to work the puppets in front of the scenery.

756 Basic Stick Puppet

Cut a medium-sized picture from a magazine. Glue the picture to a piece of posterboard and trim around the edges. Cover the picture with clear self-stick paper, if desired. Glue a craft stick handle to the back of the posterboard.

 ## 757 Character Stick Puppet

Cut a hat shape out of felt and glue it to the top of a tongue depressor. Add felt clothing shapes and felt-tip marker features.

758 Circle Puppet

Cut two 4-inch circles out of self-stick paper. Remove the backing from one of the circles. Cut yarn into short pieces and place them around the edges of the top half of the sticky side of the circle for hair. Remove the backing from the second circle and place it on top of the first circle, sticky sides together, with a craft stick in between for a handle. Use permanent felt-tip markers to add facial features.

 ## 759 Greeting Card Puppets

Find greeting cards with pictures of animals, people or other characters on them. Cut the characters out and attach each one to a craft stick handle.

 ## 760 Shadow Puppet

Cut a shape out of posterboard. Glue a craft stick handle to the back of the shape. Hold the puppet in front of a light to make a shadow.

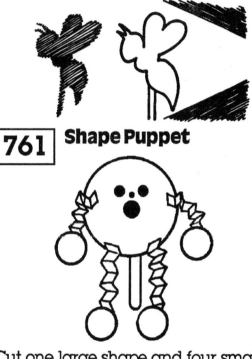

761 Shape Puppet

Cut one large shape and four smaller versions of the same shape out of construction paper. Then cut two 6-inch and two 4-inch strips out of construction paper. Fold the strips accordion style. Glue the shorter pieces to the large shape for arms and the longer pieces to the shape for legs. Attach the small shapes to the ends of the folded paper strips for hands and feet. Glue a craft stick handle to the back of the large shape. Add facial features with felt-tip markers.

762 Sticker Puppets

Make simple puppets by attaching stickers to the ends of tongue depressors. If a sticker is larger than the tongue depressor, place a plain piece of paper behind it and trim the paper to fit the sticker shape.

763 Tube Puppet

Glue construction paper facial features to the top of a cardboard toilet tissue tube. Cut short pieces of yarn and glue them around the top rim of the tube. Draw on clothing with felt-tip markers. Glue a craft stick to the inside of the tube for a handle.

More Puppets

764 Balloon Puppet

Blow up and knot a balloon. Hold the balloon by the knot and use a permanent felt-tip marker to draw facial features on it. Tie pieces of curly ribbon around the knot for hair. Then tie on a ribbon loop for a handle.

765 Bottle Puppet

Rinse and dry an empty dishwashing liquid bottle and discard the cap. Hold the bottle upside down. Glue or tape a piece of fabric around the bottle, leaving one-third of the bottle uncovered for a face. Turn the bottle right-side up. Use felt-tip markers to draw two eyes, a nose and a mouth on the face part of the bottle and glue pieces of yarn to the top of the bottle for hair.

766 Dish Mop Puppet

Hold a dish mop (available at grocery and variety stores) so that the mop part is at the top. Part the strings down the middle and flatten them. Make a puppet face on this flat area by gluing on plastic moving eyes and other facial features cut out of felt scraps.

767 Envelope Puppet

Tuck in the flap of a business-sized envelope. Place your hand inside the envelope with your fingers at one end and your thumb at the other. Indent the middle of the envelope toward your hand and fold your fingers and thumb together to make the puppet. Use felt-tip markers to draw on facial features. Open and close your hand to make the puppet talk.

768 Glove Puppets

Glue one part of a two-part self-gripping fastener to each finger of an old glove. Attach the second part of each self-gripping fastener to a pompom. Glue plastic moving eyes and other facial features to the pompoms. Use the self-gripping fasteners to attach the pompom characters to the glove.

769 Hairbrush Puppet

Cut two eye shapes, a nose shape and a mouth shape out of felt scraps. Glue the shapes to the back of a hairbrush.

770 Lemon-Lime Puppet

Remove the lid from a plastic lemon- or lime-shaped container. Stick an unsharpened pencil through the opening and tape it in place to make a handle. Cut eye, nose, mouth and ear shapes out of felt scraps. Glue the shapes on the container. Add yarn pieces for hair.

771 Paper Bag Puppet

Place a small paper bag flat on a table with the flap at the top. Use felt-tip markers to draw a face on the flap of the bag. Then decorate the puppet by gluing on construction paper limbs and other details as desired.

772 Paper Bowl Puppet

Paint the outside of a paper bowl. Poke a small hole in the bottom of the bowl. Insert a rubber band part way into the hole and knot the end on the inside of the bowl. Cut one head, two arms, two legs and a tail shape out of construction paper or felt. Trace around the rim of the bowl onto a piece of felt. Cut out the felt circle. Glue the head, arm, leg and tail shapes onto the bowl in the appropriate places. Then glue the felt circle to the bottom of the bowl. Turn the bowl upside down and hold onto the rubber band handle to work the puppet.

773 Spoon Puppet

Use felt-tip markers to draw a face on one side of a wooden spoon. Cut a circle out of fabric and make a slit in the middle. Stick the handle of the spoon through the slit. Hold the head of the puppet upside down and tape the fabric around the neck. Turn the puppet upright so that the fabric drapes over the spoon handle like a smock. Glue on pieces of yarn for hair.

774 Stuffed Animal Puppet

Cut a slit in the back of a stuffed animal and carefully remove the stuffing. Partially re-stuff the animal with polyester fiberfill. Insert your hand in the animal's back and extend your fingers into its arms and head to manipulate it like a puppet.

775 Tissue Puppet

Crumple a facial tissue into a ball around the top of one of your fingers. Drape a second tissue over the ball and secure it with a rubber band. Add a paper hat or any other details as desired. Use felt-tip markers to add facial features to the puppet.

776 Triangle Puppet

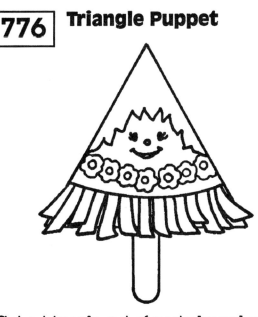

Cut a triangle out of posterboard and glue on construction paper features. Complete the puppet by attaching a craft stick handle to the back of the triangle.

777 Whisk Broom Puppet

Hold the handle of a whisk broom so that the bristles are pointing down. Cut a mouth shape and two eye shapes out of felt scraps and glue them near the top of the broom. Then cut out felt clothing shapes and glue them in the appropriate places.

Puzzles

778 Artwork Puzzles

Let the children paint or color on sheets of construction paper. Cover each child's piece of artwork on both sides with clear self-stick paper. Then cut it into three or four puzzle pieces and put the pieces in a reclosable plastic bag. Give each child his or her artwork puzzle. Let the children put their puzzles together. Then have them take their puzzles apart and put the pieces back in their bags.

779 Body Puzzle

On butcher paper, trace around your child's body. Let the child color his or her body shape. Then glue the body shape to a piece of cardboard. Cut the shape into body parts (head, arms, body and legs). Let the child put his or her body puzzle together.

780 Butterfly Puzzle

Cut a large butterfly shape out of wallpaper or construction paper. Cover the shape with clear self-stick paper and cut it into three or four puzzle pieces. Store the puzzle in a reclosable plastic bag.

781 Double-Sided Puzzle

Cut out two full-page magazine pictures. Glue the pictures on the front and back of a thin piece of cardboard. Cover the cardboard with self-stick paper and cut it into several large puzzle pieces.

782 Flannelboard Puzzle

Cut a simple familiar shape out of felt. Cut the shape into four puzzle pieces and put the pieces in a reclosable plastic bag. Let the children put the puzzle together on a flannelboard.

783 Greeting Card Puzzle

Cut a greeting card into puzzle pieces, adjusting the size and number of pieces according to the children's abilities. Put the puzzle in a reclosable plastic bag for storage.

784 Photograph Puzzle

Glue a photograph to a piece of thin cardboard. Cover it with clear self-stick paper, then cut it into three or four simple puzzle shapes.

785 Placemat Puzzles

Make a placemat puzzle for each child by cutting a piece of construction paper into two interlocking pieces. Give each child one half of a puzzle and put the other halves on a table. Let the children find the matches to their placemat halves before eating.

786 Postcard Puzzle

Cover an old picture postcard with clear self-stick paper. Cut the postcard into simple puzzle shapes and store the puzzle in an envelope.

787 Puzzle Shapes

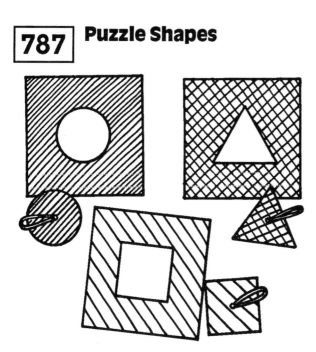

Cut three large squares out of heavy cardboard. Use a craft knife to cut a triangle out of one square, a circle out of another and a square out of the third. Push a brass paper fastener through the middle of each cutout and bend back the prongs. Wrap yarn around each paper fastener to create a loop. This allows the children to easily insert and remove the shapes.

788 Puzzle Tray

Trim a greeting card to fit inside of a plastic foam food tray before cutting it into puzzle pieces. Let the children put the puzzle together in the tray.

789 Sandwich Puzzles

Make peanut butter sandwiches. Put each sandwich on a plate and cut it into four simple puzzle pieces. Let the children put their sandwich puzzles together before eating them.

790 Storybook Puzzle

Cut a picture out of an old storybook. Cover the picture with clear self-stick paper. Then cut it into three or four pieces to create a puzzle. Store the puzzle in a reclosable plastic bag or an envelope.

791 Treasure Hunt Puzzle

Hide treats in various places around the room. Draw a picture of each place a treat is hidden. Cut each picture into four puzzle pieces. Divide the children into groups. Give each group a puzzle. Have the groups put their puzzles together to find out where their treats are hidden.

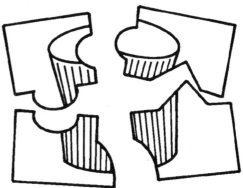

Room Props

792 Day Wheel

Cut a circle out of cardboard. Divide the circle into seven equal sections. Label each section with the name of a day of the week. Cut out a rectangular piece of cardboard, divide it into three sections and label the sections "Yesterday," "Today" and "Tomorrow." Hang the rectangular chart on a bulletin board with the circle beside it so that the current day of the week falls across the "Today" section. Rotate the wheel each day and have the children tell you what today is as well as what day yesterday was and what day tomorrow will be.

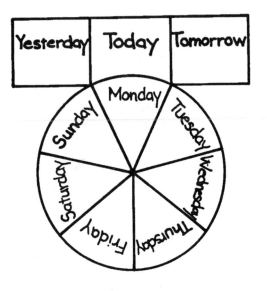

793 Health Chart

Cover a piece of cardboard with self-stick paper. Use permanent felt-tip markers to draw pictures of healthy habits you wish to reinforce (washing hands, drinking water, brushing teeth, etc.). Let the children use washable felt-tip markers to put check marks under the tasks they did that day.

794 Helper Chart

Use colored vinyl tape or masking tape to divide a piece of pegboard into as many rows as you have jobs. Hang up the pegboard and put several hooks in each row. Write each child's name on a cardboard tag with a hole punched in the top. Store each tag on a hook at the lower edge of the pegboard. To designate the day's helpers, hang the name tags in the appropriate job sections.

Feed Fish	Sue	Luis		
Water Plants	Mike			
Wash Tables	Tony	Maria	Lyle	
Feed. Hamsters	Kim			
Choose Story	Jorgé	Tom		

795 Month Wheel

Cut a large circle out of posterboard and divide it into twelve sections. Label each section with the name of a month and decorate it with a seasonal picture or sticker. (Old calendar pictures work great.) Hang the month wheel on a bulletin board. Rotate the wheel each month so that the current month appears at the top.

796 | Reusable Calendar

February						
S	M	T	W	Th	F	S
						1
2	3	4	5	6	7	8
9	10	11	12	13	14	15
16	17	18	19	20	21	22
23	24	25	26	27	28	

Draw a month grid on a large piece of cardboard. Cover the cardboard with clear self-stick paper. Write the name of the month and the dates in the appropriate places with a crayon. Wipe off the crayon with a dry paper towel to reuse the calendar.

797 | Season Wheel

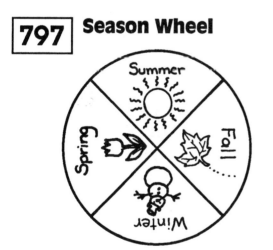

Cut a circle out of cardboard. Divide the circle into four sections. Label each section with the name of a season and decorate it with a seasonal sticker or picture. Hang the season wheel on a bulletin board. Rotate the wheel each season so that the current season is at the top. Use with the month wheel described in prop 795.

798 | Weather Chart

Use masking tape to divide a piece of pegboard into a calendar grid. Put a hook in each section of the calendar. Cut index cards to fit in the sections. Punch a hole in the top of each card. Each day set out five cards, one for each type of weather (sunny, cloudy, windy, rainy and snowy). Let the children decide which card to hang on the weather chart for that day.

799 | Weather Wheel

Cut a circle out of poster-board. Divide it into five sections. Label each section to indicate a different kind of weather (sunny, cloudy, rainy, windy and snowy) and decorate it with pictures depicting the weather condition. Attach a cardboard arrow to the center of the circle with a brass paper fastener. Let the children move the arrow to the weather for the day.

Room Props

800 Work Area Chart

Divide a piece of pegboard into sections with masking tape or colored vinyl tape. Label each section with the name of a designated work area. Hang up the pegboard and put the desired number of hooks in each section. Write each child's name on a cardboard tag with a hole punched in the top. Store each tag on a hook at the lower edge of the pegboard. Let each child come up and place his or her name tag on a hook in one of the work sections. When all the hooks in that work area have been filled, the next child must put his or her tag in another area.

Cubbies

801 Bucket Cubbies

Cover cardboard ice cream buckets with self-stick paper. Write a child's name on the inside front of each bucket. Stack the buckets and tape them together. Let the children use their buckets to store personal items.

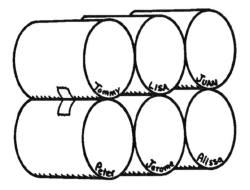

802 Shoe Bag Cubbies

Hang up a plastic shoe bag. Label each shoe pocket with a child's name. Use the pockets to hold artwork or notes to take home.

803 Storage Box Cubbies

Purchase large cardboard shoe storage boxes that are divided into sections. Label a section for each child.

Decorations

804 Decoration Tree

Find a nicely shaped bare tree branch. Spray-paint it white, if desired. Hang it on a wall or set it in a can filled with dirt, sand or cement. Decorate it with such seasonal favors as red hearts, green shamrocks, Easter eggs, spring flowers, fall leaves or small wrapped presents.

805 Glitter Vase

Paint the outside of a vase with glue. Sprinkle glitter all over the glue. Allow the glue to dry. Use the vase to display flowers, small tree branches or other nature items.

806 Leather-Look Vase
Select a fancy-shaped jar or bottle. Cover the jar entirely with torn pieces of masking tape. Paint over the covered jar with brown liquid shoe polish to create a leather look.

Displays

807 Cardboard Box Display
Cut off the top, bottom and one side of a cardboard box. Set it on a table and use it to display objects and pictures about a specific theme.

808 Corkboard Display
Attach squares of corkboard to the walls at the children's eye level. Hang pictures relating to current teaching topics on the corkboard.

809 Fabric-Covered Display
Cover a large piece of cardboard with fabric or wallpaper. Add a fabric or wallpaper border, if desired.

810 Parent Message Board
Place a message board where parents will see it when they pick up or visit their children. Corkboard works best, but a piece of plasterboard or heavy cardboard covered with fabric or self-stick paper can also be used.

811 Plasterboard
Tape the edges of a piece of plasterboard. Prop the board against a wall to use.

Play Equipment

812 Cardboard Playhouse
Cut off the top and bottom flaps of a large cardboard box. Cut out a door on one side and windows on the other sides to make a simple playhouse.

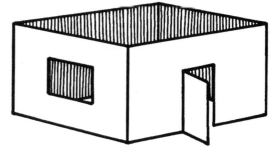

813 Feelie Room
Turn a large cardboard box into a feelie room. Cut off the top and bottom flaps of a large cardboard box. Cut a door in one side. Line the inside of the box with different textured materials such as corrugated cardboard, sandpaper, crepe paper, aluminum foil, fabric, cotton balls, cotton batting, vinyl and plastic bubble packing material.

814 Mirror House

Cut off the top and bottom flaps of a large cardboard box. Cut a door in one side. Line the inside of the box with reflective materials such as mirrors, aluminum foil and foil wallpaper. Add shiny hubcaps, old coffee pots and toasters to your mirror house.

815 Play Store

Remove the back of a large cardboard box and cut a window in the front. Have a child stand behind the window and pretend to be the cashier at your play store.

816 Puppet Theater

Remove the back of a large cardboard box and cut a window in the front to create a puppet stage. Decorate the puppet theater with paint and construction paper as desired.

Quiet Area Props

817 Bathtub

If you have access to an old bathtub (look for one at a junk yard), set it up in your reading area. Fill the tub with colorful pillows. Let two children at a time crawl into the tub and read their favorite books.

818 Couch

Set up an old clean couch (look for one at thrift shops) in your reading area. Let the children sit on the couch if they are actively "reading" a book from your library.

819 Hula-Hoop Tepee

Tape a Hula-Hoop to the floor. Hang a bent coat hanger from the ceiling. Run string or heavy yarn from the hoop to the hanger as shown in the illustration. Cover the yarn frame with a large piece of fabric, a sheet or a lightweight blanket.

820 Large Box

Tape the sides of a large, sturdy box securely together. Cut a door and a window into one side of the box. Place brightly colored pillows into the box and let the children use the area as a quiet reading or "thinking" spot.

Room Dividers

 Bulletin Board Divider
Nail a two-by-four to each side of a large bulletin board to make a movable room divider.

 Cardboard Box Divider
Cut off the top and bottom of a 3-foot-high cardboard box. Cut the box apart at one corner. Cover both sides of the cardboard with self-stick paper. Stand the cardboard on end to make a room divider.

 Cupboard Dividers
Place low cupboards in the middle of the room rather than along the walls to divide work areas.

 Fabric Divider
Attach hinges to three 4-foot-high wooden frames. Stretch fabric across the bottom halves of the frames and staple it in place.

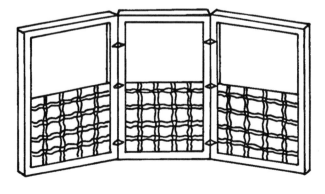

Tents

 Card Table Tent
Cover an old card table with sheets, blankets or large pieces of fabric. Place big, fluffy pillows inside the tent and let the children use the space for a hide-a-way.

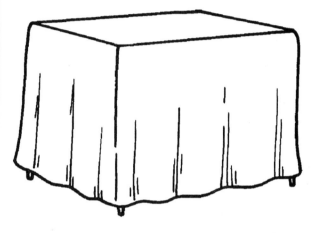

826 **Chair Tent**
Slip the corners of a fitted sheet over the backs of four chairs that are of equal height. Or drape light-weight blankets over the backs of the chairs.

827 **Climber Tent**
Cover an indoor or outdoor climber with fabric, sheets or blankets and let the children use the climber as a hide-out. If you wish to use the area as a quiet spot, you may need to re-strict its climbing use.

828 **Pup Tent**
Set up a two-person, self-standing pup tent inside for a quiet area. Place soft pillows or an air mattress inside the tent.

Sand Props

Indoor Sandboxes

 829 **Bathtub Sandbox**
Find an old bathtub that is no longer being used. Place it in a corner of the room and fill it with sand.

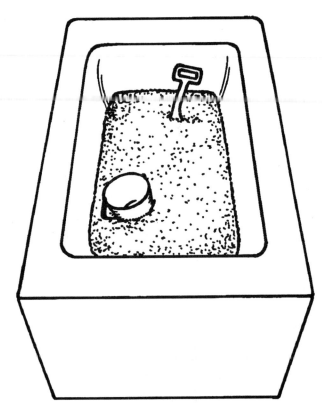

 830 **Dishpan Sandbox**
Line a dishpan with a small plastic trash bag. Pour in several inches of sand. To store the sand, pick up the bag, fasten it with a twist tie and keep it in a dry place.

 831 **Rainy Day Sandbox**
To make a small indoor sandbox, cut the sides down on a sturdy cardboard box so that they are about 5 inches high. Fill the box half full with sand. Do not expect children to share a small box.

 **832** **Sand Pool**

Recycle an old, plastic wading pool with slight cracks or holes in it. Patch cracks or holes with duct tape. Spread a large dropcloth on the floor, place the plastic pool on top and fill it with sand.

Sand Substitutes

833 **Coffee Grounds**
Collect 4 cups washed and dried coffee grounds. Mix in 1 cup flour and 2 cups cornmeal.

834 **Cornstarch**
Mix two boxes of cornstarch with just enough water to make it thick and smooth. Color the mixture with food coloring, if desired.

835 Dried Beans

To create a fall atmosphere in your sand table, fill it with dried black beans and dried chick peas.

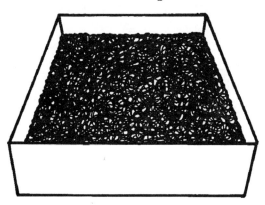

836 Macaroni

Dye elbow macaroni pastel colors to give a springtime look to your sand table. Add a large amount of food coloring to a small amount of water and let the noodles soak until they are the desired shade. Allow the macaroni to dry. Then put it in the sand table with colored plastic eggs for scoops.

837 Rainbow Rice

Mix food coloring with cold water and add uncooked white rice. Let the rice soak in the water until it is the desired color. Make several colors of rice, allow them to dry and then mix them together in the sand table for a rainbow effect.

838 Sand Substitute Fun

Use any of the following items as sand substitutes in the sand table: birdseed, cornmeal, crumbled cork, dry cereal, pasta or salt.

Sand Table Props

839 Basic Sand Table Props

Set out a variety of the items listed below for the children to use at the sand table.

- cardboard tubes
- gelatin molds
- measuring cups
- measuring spoons
- plastic containers
- plastic tubing
- scoops
- spatulas
- spoons
- tongue depressors
- toy cars
- toy people

840 Big Sand Funnel

Screw four eye hooks into the ceiling in a square shape above the sand table. Poke four evenly-spaced holes around the rim of a large plastic funnel. Attach a thin rope to each hole. Tie each rope to one of the eye hooks. Adjust the ropes so that the tip of the funnel is 4 to 6 inches above the sand in the sand table. Let the children fill the funnel with sand and swing it around to make sand designs.

841 Can Sieve

Use a nail to punch holes in the top or sides of an empty plastic tennis ball container to make a sieve.

842 Creative Sand Play Props

Keep a large container filled with props for creative sand play. Let the children choose from a variety of items listed below.

- birthday candles
- cardboard tubes
- cookie cutters
- flags
- large buttons
- pine cones
- plastic people
- seashells
- spatulas
- straws
- toy cars
- walnut shells

843 Dishwashing Liquid Bottle Funnel

Cut the bottom off of a plastic dishwashing liquid bottle. Cover all sharp edges with tape. Turn the top half upside down and let the children use it for a funnel in the sand table.

844 Measuring Can

Use a Parmesan cheese container in the sand table. The children can learn by experience the concepts of more and less by rotating the top for different pouring amounts.

845 Pie Pan Sand Sieve

Use a nail to poke holes in the bottom of an aluminum pie pan. Smooth out any sharp edges.

846 Plastic Bleach Bottle Funnel

Cut a large plastic bleach bottle in half. Cover all sharp edges with tape. Turn the top half upside down and let the children use it for a funnel in the sand table.

847 Sand Comb

Cut "teeth" on one side of a heavy cardboard rectangle. Let the children use the sand comb to make interesting designs in the sand.

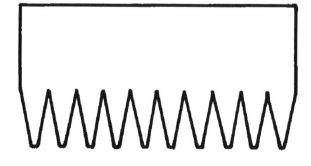

848 Sand Pail

Attach a rope handle to the top of a cardboard ice cream bucket. Cover the container with colorful self-stick paper.

849 Sand Sifters

Use a nail to poke several holes in the bottoms of margarine tubs or whipped topping containers. Vary the size and number of holes as desired.

850 Sock-Dozer

Fill an old athletic sock with 1 ½ cups of sand. Tie the top of the sock into a knot or tie a piece of twine around the top. Let the children drag the sock in the sand to make ditches and designs.

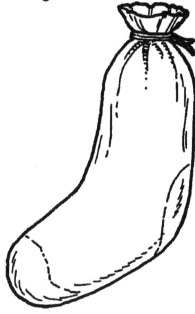

851 Spray Bottles

Fill spray bottles with water. Let the children spray water on the sand to keep it damp and easier to mold.

852 Water

Add water to the sand in the sand table. Let the children play in the wet sand. To dry the sand, leave the cover off the sand table for a few days.

Science Props

Animal Props

853 Use a craft knife to cut two 2- to 3-inch holes directly across from each other in a plastic soft-drink bottle. Use a hole punch to make a small hole 1 inch below each larger hole. Insert a 7-inch piece of ¼-inch wooden dowel through the two small holes. Use a nail to poke two holes across from each other near the top of the bottle. Thread a piece of twine through the holes to make a hanger. Fill the bottom of the bottle with birdseed.

854 **Bird Feeder Carton**
Cut out a large window in one side of a half-gallon cardboard milk carton. Tape the top of the carton closed and poke a hole in the middle of it. Thread a piece of twine through the hole to make a hanger. Fill the carton up to the level of the window with bird seed.

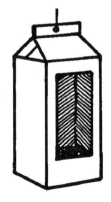

855 **Earthworm Farm**
Fill a wooden frame with earthworm bedding material purchased from a sporting goods store. (Or make your own bedding material by mixing potting soil with sphagnum moss and a sprinkling of cornmeal.) Add worms you have collected from other locations. To feed the worms, dust the bedding material with cornmeal from time to time.

Flying Props

856 **Airplane**

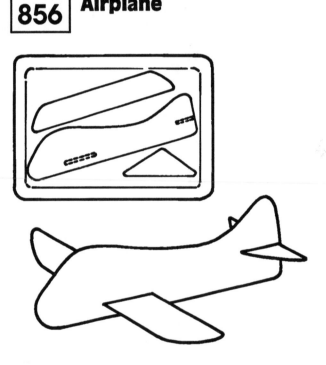

Draw an airplane body shape, a wings shape and a tail shape on a plastic foam food tray. (See illustration.) Cut out the shapes and make slits in the airplane body as indicated by the dotted lines. Insert the wings shape through the wide slit in the airplane body and the tail shape in the notched slit in the back.

857 Parachute

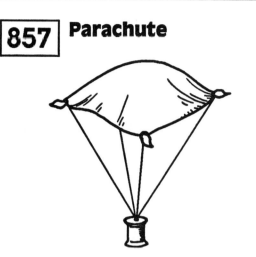

Cut four 12-inch pieces of string. Tie the strings to the corners of an old handkerchief or fabric square, one string on each corner. Then thread the ends of the strings through the hole in an empty spool. Tie the ends in a knot too big to slip back through the hole. Toss the parachute up into the air and watch it float down to the ground.

858 Rocket

Thread a length of string through a straw. Have two children hold the string tightly between them. Blow up a balloon and have another child hold the end closed while you tape the side of the balloon to the straw as shown. When you say, "Go," have the child let go of the end of the balloon to make it "rocket" along the string.

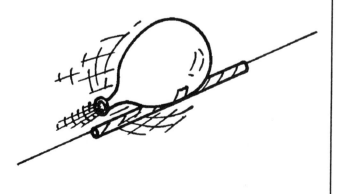

859 Ant Farm Box

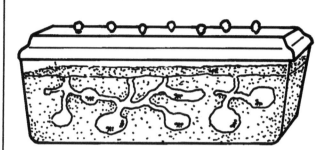

Carefully collect several ants and some dirt or sand. Let the ants calm down for a few minutes, then put them into a large clear plastic box (the kind that shoes are stored in). Heat the sharp end of a nail and press it against the box lid to make a hole. Make several holes. Fill the holes with cotton and tape the lid securely to the box. Let the children observe the industrious ants, but be sure to cover the box with a cloth when the ants are not being observed. (This keeps the ants from digging deep tunnels to escape the light.) Once a week, let the children place a small amount of jelly, fruit or honey mixed with water through one of the holes, removing the cotton first and replacing it after feeding. Every three days have them add about a teaspoon of water through one of the holes with an eyedropper. When the children's study of ants is over, return the tiny creatures to their natural habitat.

860 Bug House

Cut a rectangle out of each side of a clean half-gallon cardboard milk carton. Tape the top closed. Collect one or two insects. Put the insects, along with some grass and twigs, in the milk carton. Cover the carton with an old nylon stocking and use a twist tie to fasten the nylon around the top of it. Observe the insects inside. Carefully return the insects to the area where they were found when you are done observing them.

861 Bug Keeper

Cut a 7- by 9-inch rectangle out of soft wire screening material. Collect two identical plastic spray can lids. Roll the screening into a cylinder that fits snugly into one of the lids. Sew the screening in place. Cover any remaining sharp edges with masking tape. Put the cylinder in one of the lids. Use the cylinder to catch a bug, then place the second lid on the open end. Observe the bug through the screening. Release the bug in the area where it was found when you are done.

862 Butterfly Garden

Put some twigs and pieces of grass in a canning jar. Poke small air holes in the jar lid. Put a caterpillar in the jar and screw on the lid. Watch the caterpillar spin a chrysalis (or cocoon) and evolve into a butterfly (or moth). Open the jar and watch the butterfly flutter away outdoors.

863 Individual Ant Farms

Purchase small clear-plastic containers with lids. Punch holes in the tops of the containers and write a child's name on each one. Let each child collect and feed the ants as described in prop 859.

Magnet Props

864 Magic Magnet Jar

Fill a jar with water and place a paper clip in it. Make the paper clip dance up and down in the water by moving a magnet up and down the outside of the jar. The paper clip moves because the magnetic force passes through the glass and the water to the paper clip.

865 Magnetic Dowels

Stand small sections of dowels in playdough bases. Set out several donut-shaped magnets. Show the children how to put the magnets on the dowels so that they stick together. Then show them how to put the magnets on the dowels so that the magnets repel or push away from each other.

866 Magnetic Sorting Boxes

Set out a magnet, two boxes and various small magnetic and non-magnetic objects such as a paper clip, a screw, a button, a piece of chalk, a piece of aluminum foil, a spoon, a kitchen magnet and a safety pin. Label one box with a picture of a magnet and the words "Things that stick." Label the other box with the words "Things that don't stick." Let the children take turns selecting an object, testing to see if it sticks to the magnet, then putting it in the appropriate box.

Plant Props

867 Egg Carton Nursery

Place empty eggshell halves in the cups of an egg carton. Fill the shells with potting soil. Plant one or two radish or carrot seeds in each shell and add a teaspoon of water to each one.

Keep the egg carton closed so that the seeds will stay warm and sprout more quickly. After the seeds have sprouted and grown into seedlings, plant the eggshells outside, crushing them slightly before placing them in the ground.

868 Hydroponic Garden

Poke a hole in the bottom of a short, wide-mouthed plastic cup. Put a ¼- by 3-inch strip of sponge through the hole. Mix water and liquid plant food in a watering can according to the directions on the plant food bottle. Fill a tall narrow-mouthed plastic cup partway with water from the watering can. Carefully place the short cup on top of the tall cup so that the sponge strip hangs down into the water. Fill the short cup with vermiculite. Plant lettuce or bean seeds in the vermiculite and set the cups in a sunny location. Add the water and fertilizer mixture to the tall cup as necessary. (Caution: Children need adult supervision at all times while working with fertilizer.)

869 Jar Terrarium

Put a layer of small rocks and two or three inches of potting soil in a jar with a lid. Plant one or two small plants in the soil. Use an eyedropper to add a small amount of water to the plants. Screw the lid on the jar.

870 Planter Cup

Fill a paper cup with dirt. Plant two or three fast-growing seeds, such as nasturtium seeds or bean seeds, in the cup. Water the seeds as necessary.

871 Spray Bottle

Fill a spray bottle with water. Let the children use the spray bottle to water the plants around the room.

872 Sprout Bag

Use a needle to punch tiny holes in the bottom of a sandwich-sized reclosable plastic bag. Be sure that some of the holes are on the bottom seam so that water will drain well from the bag. Fill the bag about one-eighth full with alfalfa or mung bean seeds. Close the bag and place it in a bowl of warm water. Soak the seeds overnight. The next day, drain the seeds well and place them in a sunny place, but not in direct sunlight. Rinse and drain the seeds daily for three to four days. Place the sprouted seeds in direct sunlight on the last day and they will green-up more. Store the sprouts in the same bag in the refrigerator.

873 Plastic Cup Terrarium

Put a layer of small rocks and two or three inches of potting soil in a clear-plastic cup. Plant one or two small plants in the soil. Use an eye-dropper to add a small amount of water to the plants. Place a second plastic cup upside down on top of the first one and tape the cups together.

874 Seed Viewing Jar

Line a glass jar with two or three wet paper towels. Fill the jar with 1 inch of water. Place bean seeds between the paper towels and the jar. Place the glass in a warm, dark place. Take the jar out daily to observe the seeds. Add water as needed to keep it at the 1-inch level. (Hint: To keep the paper towels firmly against the glass and seeds, crumple up more wet paper towels and stuff them into the jar.

Recycling Props

875 Aluminum Can Crusher

Attach a hinge between two 2-foot sections of two-by-fours so that the pieces stack on top of each other and open and close. Lift up one of the wood pieces and nail a mayonnaise jar lid to the bottom one, about 12 inches from the hinge. To use, lift up the top piece, place a can in the mayonnaise jar lid and close it back down as far as possible to crush the can.

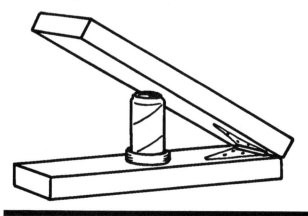

876 Commercial Can Crusher

Purchase a commercial aluminum can crusher and mount it on the wall next to your aluminum can recycling box. Let the children take turns crushing cans with it.

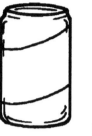

877 Recycling Station

Collect one box for each item you want to recycle, such as glass, aluminum cans, newspaper, mixed paper, plastic, etc. Paint the boxes in bright colors and line them up against a wall.

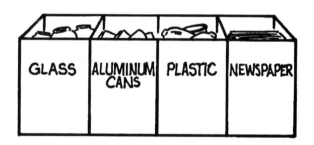

878 Reusable Paper Box

Cover an empty cardboard box with self-stick paper. Place the box next to a garbage can or a paper recycling box. Have the children put papers in the box that they no longer want and that are only marked on one side. Then encourage the children to look in the reusable paper box when they want paper to draw on or to use in art projects.

879 Worm Composting Bin

Line a sturdy cardboard box with plastic. Make ten small holes in the bottom of the box for drainage. Fill the box with a bedding material such as grass, peat moss or straw. Add some red worms (available at bait shops). Keep the bedding material moist. Feed the worms any leftover food scraps except meat, fat and bones. When the original bedding material is no longer recognizable, push it over to one side of the box and add new bedding material. In about a week, after the worms have moved to the new material, carefully scoop out the composted material and use it to fertilize a flower or vegetable garden.

Tools

880 Glass Jar Magnifier

Fill a clear glass jar halfway with water. Place small objects in the water and look at them through the glass. The objects will look slightly larger. Or place the objects beside the jar and look at them through the jar of water. The objects will look even bigger.

881 Infant Scale

Let the children use an infant scale to weigh dolls and stuffed animals.

882 Kaleidoscope

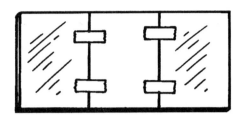

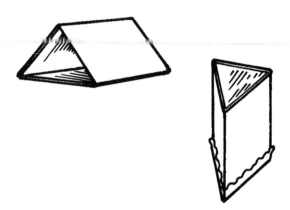

Collect the following materials: two identical oblong, travel-sized mirrors; cardboard; pencil; scissors; masking tape; waxed paper and small nature objects. Place one of the mirrors on the cardboard, trace around it and cut out the shape. Arrange the mirrors face down on a flat surface and place the piece of cardboard between them. Fasten the sides together with masking tape. Stand the mirrors and cardboard up so that they form a triangle with the mirrors facing inside. Tape the remaining sides together. Tape a piece of waxed paper over one of the ends. The kaleidoscope is now ready to use. Place two or three small nature items on the waxed paper. Have the children hold the kaleidoscope and look down into it to see six reflections of the items. Gently shake the kaleidoscope to move the items and change the reflections.

883 Kitchen Scale

Set out a kitchen scale. Let the children use the scale to weigh a variety of foods and objects from the kitchen.

884 Magnifying Glasses

Have on hand one or more good magnifying glasses. The better the quality of the magnifying glass, the safer the tool and the more gained by the children. Reasonably good magnifying glasses can be purchased at drugstores or variety stores at a nominal cost.

885 Paper Cup Balance

Cut the middle section out of the bottom of a wire coat hanger and cover the sharp ends with masking tape. Punch two holes in the rims of each of two paper cups. Attach a 6-inch piece of string to the holes in each of the cups. Hang the cups from the cut ends of the coat hanger and bend up the ends of the hanger to keep the cups from falling off. Place the top of the hanger on one finger and put a small object in each cup. Have the children tell you which item is heavier.

886 Periscope

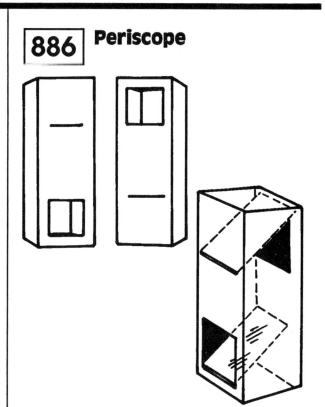

Find two identical oblong, travel-sized mirrors; a small rectangular cracker or cookie box; a craft knife; a ruler and some masking tape. Use the craft knife to cut a slit across one side of the cracker box, 2 inches from the top. On the same side, cut out a 2-inch square near the bottom. On the opposite side, cut a slit 2 inches from the bottom of the box and a 2-inch square near the top. Insert one mirror through the top slit so that it extends from the slit to the top of the box. Insert the other mirror through the bottom slit so that it extends from the slit to the bottom of the box. (The reflective sides of the mirrors should face each other.) Tape the mirrors securely in place. The periscope is now ready to use. Let the children take turns looking through one of the square openings to see the view from the other opening. Show them how to use the periscope to see around corners and over furniture.

887 Rock Sorter

Collect a sturdy shoebox and lid. Use a craft knife to cut five holes of varying sizes in the lid. Place the lid on the box. Set out the box and a number of different sized rocks. Have the children sort the rocks by placing each one in the hole closest to its size.

888 Scale

Set out a bathroom scale. Let the children use the scale to weigh a variety of heavy objects from around the room. Or have them weigh themselves on the scale.

Weather Props

889 Coffee Can Rain Gauge

Tape a ruler inside of an empty coffee can. Place the can outside where it will catch the rain. After a big rain, have the children help you check how many inches of rain fell.

890 Cloud Jar

Find a clear glass half-gallon or gallon bottle and a cork or rubber stopper that fits in its mouth. Poke a hole vertically through the stopper. Rinse the bottle with warm water and immediately insert the stopper. Blow as much air as possible into the bottle through the hole in the stopper. Cover the hole with a finger. Pull the stopper out quickly and let the children watch as a cloud forms inside the bottle. The cloud forms because there was a change from high air pressure (when the bottle was filled with air) to low air pressure (when the stopper was removed).

891 Condensation Jars

Collect two jars with lids. Fill one of the jars with ice water and the other one with room-temperature water. Screw the lids on tightly. Set the jars on a table. Ask the children to describe what is happening to the outsides of the jars. Point out that only the jar with ice water inside has drops of water on the outside. This is called condensation. Condensation happens when the water particles in the air become cold enough to change into drops of water.

892 Outdoor Thermometer

Place a large outdoor thermometer in a spot where the children can easily see it. Have the children check the temperature on the thermometer throughout the day.

893 Plastic Cup Rain Gauge

Mark inches and half-inches on the outside of a clear-plastic cup with a permanent felt-tip marker. Place the cup outside where it will catch the rain. After a big rain, have the children help you check how many inches of rain fell.

894 Rain Cycle Jar

Fill a jar partway with water and screw on its lid. Use a permanent felt-tip marker to mark the level of the water in the jar. Place the jar in a sunny window. Have the children observe the jar over the next few days as the heat from the sun warms up the water in the jar so that some of it evaporates and collects at the top of the jar. This demonstrates how the rain cycle works.

895 Rain Maker

Fill a saucepan with water and bring it to a boil over a stove or a hot plate. Fill a pie pan with ice cubes. Have the children stand or sit where they can see the pan of boiling water and the steam that is forming above it. Use a hot pad to hold the pie pan filled with ice cubes over the steam "cloud." Have the children observe that when the steam comes in contact with the cool air from the pie pan, drops of water form and fall back into the saucepan like rain. This is similar to the way rain is really made. (Caution: Adults should always supervise activities that require electrical appliances.)

896 Rainbow Maker

Place a small mirror in a glass or water and tilt it against the side of the glass. Then stand the glass in direct sunlight so that the mirror reflects a rainbow on a wall.

897 Snow Gauge

Use the coffee can rain gauge in prop 889 or the plastic cup rain gauge in prop 893 to measure a snowfall.

898 Thermometer

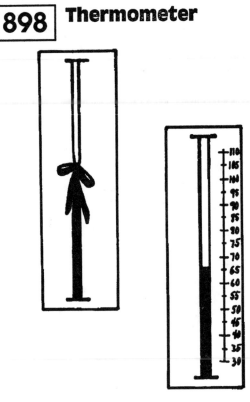

Make a thermometer for the children to play with. Cut a small, narrow rectangle out of cardboard. Hold the rectangle with one of the short sides up. Make a horizontal slit near the top and the bottom of the rectangle. Mark the front of the rectangle with degrees to resemble a thermometer. Cut a piece of white ribbon that is slightly more than twice as long as the rectangle. Color half of the ribbon red. Thread the ribbon through the slits and tie the ends together in the back of the thermometer. Show the children how to move the ribbon up and down to make the temperature reading change.

899 Bag Kite

Decorate a small bag with crayons or felt-tip markers. Punch a hole on the top side of the bag near the opening and tie a piece of yarn through the hole. Have a child hold onto the yarn and run to make the bag kite fill with air and fly up and down.

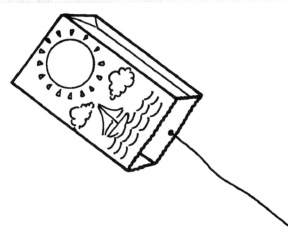

900 Paper Plate Kite

Glue strips of crepe paper to one end of a paper plate. Tie a yarn handle to the opposite side of the plate. Let a child hold onto the yarn handle and run with the paper plate kite to make it fly.

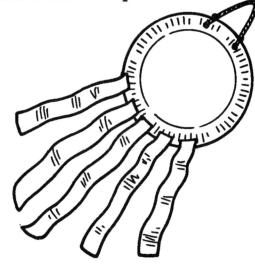

901 Pinwheel

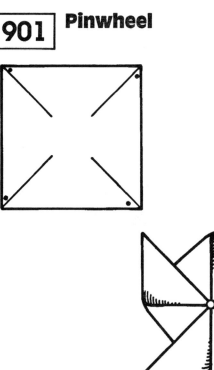

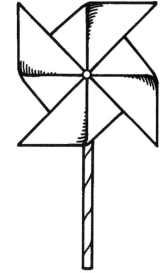

Cut a large square out of construction paper. Make four cuts in the square as shown in the illustration. Bring four of the corners, indicated by the dots, to the center of the square. Hold the corners in place with a brass paper fastener. Attach the pinwheel to a straw.

902 Straws

Give each child a straw. Let the children experiment with using the straws to blow lightweight items across a tabletop or other flat surface. Then show them how to use their straws to pick up small pieces of paper by placing one of the ends of their straws on the papers and sucking on the other ends.

903 Wind Catcher

Cut a vertical "door" in each side of a half-gallon cardboard milk carton. (Make sure the doors are cut so that they will all open in the same direction.) Fold the doors open. Punch a hole in the top of the carton and tie a piece of string through it. Hang the wind catcher outside and watch it twirl.

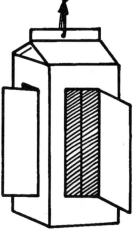

904 Wind Hummer

Cut the rim off a plastic lid. Use a nail to punch two holes, 1 inch apart, in the center of the circle. Thread a 16-inch piece of string through the holes and tie the ends together. Give a child the wind hummer. Show the child how to "wind up" the circle by moving the strings in a circular motion. Then have the child pull the string tight to make the circle hum.

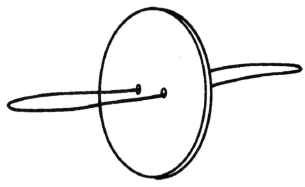

905 Windsock

Remove the top and bottom of an oatmeal box or a salt box and cover it with construction paper. Staple strips of crepe paper to the bottom edge of the box. Punch four holes in the top of the box. Lace a string knotted at one end through each hole and tie the four loose ends together. Hang the windsock outside and watch it move in the wind.

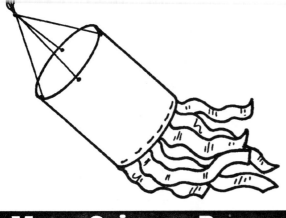

More Science Props

906 Candle Clock

Place two candles that are the same length in candle holders. Burn one candle for 30 minutes. Measure the difference in length between the two candles. Then use that measurement to mark lines down the side of the unburned candle. Set the first candle aside and light the marked candle while the children watch. Explain that when the candle burns down to the first line, 30 minutes will have gone by; when it burns down to the second line, another 30 minutes (or 60 minutes) will have gone by, etc. Then let the children periodically check the candle as it burns. (Caution: Activities that involve lighted candles require adult supervision at all times.)

907 Crystal Jar

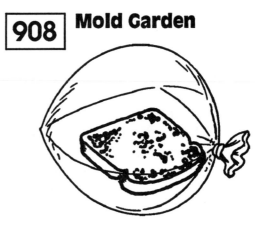

Mix 1 tablespoon Epsom salt and 1 tablespoon water in a baby food jar. Then stir in ¼ teaspoon of red, blue or green food coloring. Over the next few days, the water in the jar will evaporate and small crystals will begin to form.

908 Mold Garden

Sprinkle a piece of bread with 1 teaspoon of water and put the bread in a clear plastic bag. Blow up the bag and close it securely with a twist tie. Then place the bag in a warm dark place. After five or six days, little mold spots will begin appearing on the bread. Keep the bag closed and let the children observe as the mold continues to grow. At the end of the project, throw out the unopened bag.

909 Sand Timer

Make a sand timer using two baby food jars and lids. Glue the lids together back-to-back. (Use glue made for adhering to metal.) Allow the glue to dry overnight. Carefully use a hammer and a large nail to punch several holes in the lids. Fill one of the jars with sand and put on the lids. Screw the empty jar on top of the filled jar. Tip the jars over and time how long it takes for the sand to stop running. By adding or removing sand, you can adjust the sand in the timer to run a certain amount of time such as one or two minutes.

910 Star Scope

Tape a black construction paper circle over one end of a cardboard toilet tissue tube. Gently punch holes in the paper with a toothpick. To use the star scope, have a child hold the scope up to the light and look through the uncovered end. The light will shine through the holes, creating a miniature planetarium.

911 Volcano

For this volcano you will need a small peat pot (available at most nurseries). Place the peat pot upside down in a pan of water to soften the top. Push the softened top down to form a crater. Set the volcano on a cookie sheet or flat surface outside. Next to the volcano place two baby food jars, one filled with baking soda and one filled with vinegar. Have the children take turns spooning a little baking soda into the crater, then using an eye dropper to add drops of vinegar to make the volcano "erupt."

Storytime Props

Puppet Stages

912 Doorway Puppet Stage

Attach two curtain rod holders to the wall on either side of a door frame at the desired height. Cut a piece of vinyl or sailcloth the width of the door and 3 inches taller than the height of the rod holders. Make a 3-inch hem at the top of the fabric. Slide the curtain rod through the hem and hang the rod on the holders. Have the audience sit on one side of the curtain while the puppeteers sit or stand on the other side and operate their puppets.

913 Finger Puppet Stage

Turn an empty pop-up facial tissue box on its side. Cut off what is now the bottom of the box. Hold the box so that the cut-out opening is at the bottom and the pop-up opening is facing forward. Put finger puppets on one hand and stick your hand up into the box so that the puppets show through the pop-up opening.

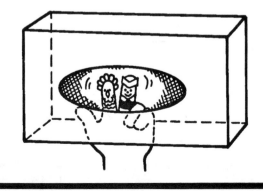

914 Paper Plate Puppet Stage

Cut a horizontal slit in the center of a paper plate. Cover each side of the slit with tape to prevent paper cuts. Make a 1-inch vertical cut at each end of the slit. Draw a background scene on the paper plate. Insert a finger puppet through the slit to perform "on stage."

915 Stick Puppet Stage

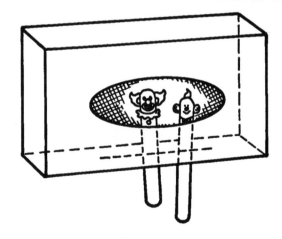

Turn an empty pop-up facial tissue box on its side and cut a slit in the new bottom of the box. Insert stick puppets up through the slits and into the box so that they show through the pop-up opening.

916 Story Candle

Have the children sit with you around a low table. Set a candle on the table. Light the candle and turn out the lights in the room. Have the children focus on the candle while you tell a short story. Encourage the children to imagine pictures for the story. If desired, a flashlight can be used in place of the candle. (Caution: Activities that involve a lighted candle require adult supervision at all times.)

917 Story Chest

Find a small interesting-looking chest and fill it with such story props as an old hat, a lantern, a toy fire engine, a stuffed animal and a blanket. Before you read a story, look through the chest, select an item that relates to your story and show it to the children.

918 Story Hats

Find an old, large hat box. Put a hat that relates to a story in the box. Before you read the story, open the box to reveal the hat. Let the children tell you what kind of hat it is and guess who might wear it. Then tell them how the hat fits into the story.

919 Story Mobile

Make a simple mobile by hanging different lengths of yarn from a wire coat hanger or from a plastic lid with the middle cut out. Attach paper cutouts of a story's characters to the yarn. Hang up the story mobile. Use the mobile to start or review a story.

920 Double Story Cubes

Make two story cubes as described in prop 921. Have the children roll both cubes, name the persons or objects on top and make up a short story or a sentence that includes both.

921 Roll-A-Story Cube

Fill a picture cube with pictures of various objects and people. Let the children take turns rolling the cube and naming the picture that lands on top. Incorporate the person or object in the picture into a group story.

922 Story Bag

Fill a small bag with objects such as toy cars, dolls, toy furniture and stuffed or plastic animals. Let the children take turns drawing an object out of the bag. Make up a story that incorporates each object as it is drawn.

923 Story Shapes

Cut geometric shapes out of felt. Give each child a small carpet square and some of the felt shapes. Have the children use their felt shapes to create simple pictures on their carpet squares. When the children have completed their pictures, line up the carpet squares and tell a story that incorporates each picture. (To avoid embarrassment, have the children name their pictures before you start the story.)

924 Story Spinner

Divide a paper plate into eight sections. Draw a small picture in each section. Draw pictures based on a theme (objects at a birthday party, objects used in the winter, etc.) or draw objects selected at random.

Attach a spinner to the middle of the plate by putting a brass paper fastener through the bottom of a closed safety pin. Let the children take turns spinning the spinner and naming the pictured object the spinner lands on. Incorporate each object into a group story.

925 Story Tree

Create a story tree by securing a large branch in a pot of dirt, rocks or cement. Spray-paint the tree white, if desired. As you tell a story, hang small objects that represent the characters or events of the story on the tree. To make the objects easier to hang, wrap rubber bands around them and attach opened paper clips to use as hooks. Or make story characters out of felt scraps and sew on yarn loops for hanging. When the story is over, point to each character on the tree and let the children help you review the story.

926 Tube Town

Collect cardboard toilet tissue tubes and cover them with self-stick paper, if desired. Cut two 1-inch slits opposite each other in the top of each tube. Place cardboard shapes into the slits to create stand-up story characters. Set the characters out on a table and move them around as you tell a story.

Storyboard Cutouts

927 Fabric Softener Sheets

Cut simple story characters out of used sponge-type fabric softener sheets.

928 Felt

Cut simple story character shapes out of felt pieces. Add details by cutting them out of felt scraps and gluing them on the cutouts.

929 Magnetic

Cut story character shapes out of cardboard, paper, plastic foam or balsa wood scraps. Attach small strips of self-stick magnetic tape to the backs of the characters.

930 Paper

Cut pictures of characters out of magazines or old books. Mount the pictures on heavy paper, if necessary. Or draw characters on construction paper and color them with felt-tip markers or crayons. Glue strips of flannel or felt to the backs of the pictures and use them on a flannelboard.

931 Paper Towels

Create storyboard shapes easily and inexpensively by making them out of paper towels. Thick, white spongy towels work best. Use felt-tip markers to decorate the shapes, then use them on a flannelboard.

932 Carpet Storyboard
Let the children use an indoor-outdoor carpet square as a storyboard. Set out a reclosable plastic bag filled with felt cutouts. Have the children place the felt cutouts on the carpet square and make up stories about them.

 933 Cookie Sheet
Let the children use a cookie sheet as a storyboard for magnetic cutouts.

 934 Felt Story Apron
Cut a simple butcher-style apron out of felt. Sew a ribbon neck strap at the top and ribbon ties on the sides. Sew large felt pockets on the front. Place felt cutouts for a particular story in the pockets. Pull out the cutouts and place them on the apron as you tell the story.

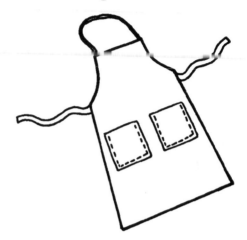

935 Magnetic Storyboard
Cover a large cookie sheet with colored self-stick paper to make a background. For example, to make an outdoor scene, cover the top half of the cookie sheet with blue self-stick paper and the bottom half with green. Or cover the entire cookie sheet with white self-stick paper and add furniture shapes cut out of other colors of self-stick paper to create an indoor scene. Place magnetic cutouts on the board as you tell a story.

936 Magnetic Flannelboard
Place lightweight wire screening between a piece of flannel and a piece of cardboard to make a magnetic flannelboard. Tape the edges closed. Use the magnetic flannelboard with felt or magnetic cutouts.

937 Room Divider Storyboards

Staple flannel or felt to the backs of bookcases, room dividers or movable storage containers to make storyboards.

938 Story Gameboards

Purchase old fold-up gameboards at garage sales and cover them with flannel. The boards are sturdy and will stand up by themselves. Make several different backgrounds and have them ready to use for favorite flannelboard stories and activities.

939 Story Shoebox

For a small individual storyboard, cut and glue a piece of felt inside the lid of a shoebox. Let the children use the lid for displaying felt character cutouts from a favorite story. Store the cutouts in the box for later use.

940 Bookcase

Use a plastic napkin holder to store small, thin storybooks.

941 Puppet Holder

Hang a pocket-type shoe organizer on a wall or a door. Store puppets in the pockets.

942 Seating Mats

Scatter small carpet squares on the floor before storytime. Have each child sit on a different square. This gives each child his or her own space and helps the children sit still longer.

943 Seating Towels

Place small towels in a circle on the floor before storytime. Have each child sit on a different towel.

944 | Story Chair

Designate a chair to be the story chair. (A rocking chair works well.) Have the person who is reading or telling the story sit in the story chair. Let the children take turns sitting in the story chair as they look through storybooks or tell their friends short stories.

945 | Story Game

Using a simple story that the children enjoy, make a gameboard with a path that passes through various scenes from the story. Use pictures copied from the storybook or draw your own. Have the children roll a die to move a marker along the path, retelling the story as they move through the scenes.

946 | Story Picture Cube

Fill a picture cube with pictures from a story. Have the children use the cube to retell the story, showing each picture in the proper order.

947 | Story Puzzle

Laminate a picture from a familiar children's storybook or cover it with clear self-stick paper. Cut the picture into three or four puzzle pieces. Set the pieces on a low table. Let the children put the puzzle together and name the story that the picture illustrates.

948 | Story Sequence Cards

Collect two copies of one of the children's favorite picture books. Cut the pages out of both books. Glue each right-hand page from one book to a piece of posterboard. Glue each left-hand page from the other book to a piece of posterboard. Cover the posterboard cards with clear self-stick paper. Use the cards to read the story to the children. Then mix up the cards and let the children put them back in the proper sequence.

949 | Story Shawl

Place a shawl around your shoulders and call it the "story shawl." Tell the children to put away their projects and go to the story area whenever they see you put on the story shawl. Let the children take turns wearing the shawl when they share stories with the group.

Water Props

950 Balloon Boat

Poke a hole in the center of a plastic foam plate. Insert the end of a balloon through the hole. Blow up the balloon and knot it. This boat is hard to tip over and it sails well in a breeze.

951 Cardboard Tube Boat

Color three cardboard toilet tissue tubes with crayons. Tie the tubes together side by side to make the boat base. Cut a slit in the side of a straw. Cut a triangular sail shape out of construction paper and slip it into the slit. Poke a small hole in the center of the middle cardboard tube and stand the straw sail in the hole.

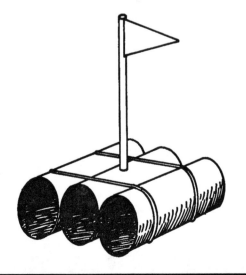

952 Cork Boat

Cut a large cork in half lengthwise. Lay one cork half on a table, flat side down. Cut a small slit into the center of the rounded side of the cork. Out of cardboard, cut a 3/4- by 1/2-inch rectangular-shaped rudder with a small tab on the top. Color both sides of the rudder with a crayon to make it waterproof. Insert the tab of the rudder into the slit in the cork.

953 Ivory Soap Boat

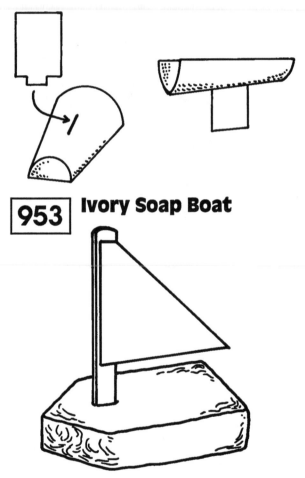

Use a craft knife to whittle one short side of a bar of Ivory soap into a point. The boat will work if it is left in the original square shape, but it will go faster with a pointed front end. Cut a sail shape out of posterboard and tape it to a craft stick. Push the craft stick into the top of the soap bar.

954 Lid Rafts

Gather several plastic lids. Cut a variety of sizes of holes out of the lids. Float the lids on the water. Let the children add play people to the boats and experiment with the number of people each raft can hold without sinking.

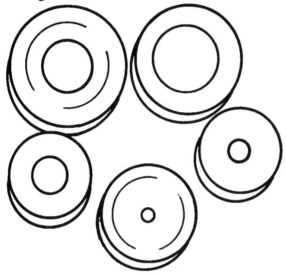

955 Milk Carton Boat

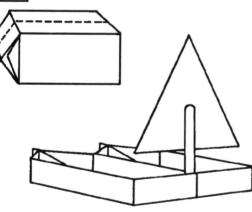

Lay a half-gallon cardboard milk carton on its side. Make a cut down the middle of the carton, leaving the bottom side intact. (See illustration.) Fold the boat open. Tape a large construction paper sail shape to a craft stick. Attach the stick to the back of the boat.

956 Plastic Foam Plate Boat

Draw a 2-inch oval boat base on a plastic foam plate. Make a small slot in the middle of the base with a craft knife. Then draw a sail-rudder shape (see illustration) on the plate. Cut the boat and sail-rudder pieces out of the plate. Place the rudder into the slot so that it points out through the bottom of the boat base and the sail sits on top of the boat.

957 Rocket Boat

Cut a half-gallon cardboard milk carton in half lengthwise and discard one half. Poke a hole in the middle of what used to be the bottom of the carton. Pull a balloon through the hole so that the end of the balloon is hanging outside the carton. (See illustration.) Have the children watch as you blow up the balloon (do not tie the end), place the boat in a bathtub or wading pool and let go of the balloon to make the boat "rocket" across the water.

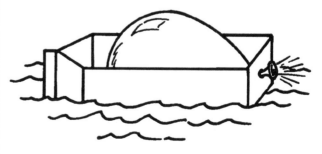

958 Soap-Powered Motor Boat

To make this boat, cut a house shape out of a plastic foam food tray. Cut a door out of the bottom of the house to complete the boat. Place the boat in a pan of water. Carefully put a few drops of liquid soap in the opening of the boat and watch it move across the water.

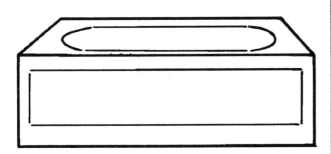

Indoor Water Tables

959 Bathtub

Fill a bathtub with water. Let two or three children kneel at the edge of the bathtub to play in the water.

960 Dishpan Water Table

Fill a dishpan with water and place it on a towel on a low table. Let a child play in the water with small water toys.

961 Infant Bathtub

Place a plastic infant bathtub on the floor and fill it partway with water.

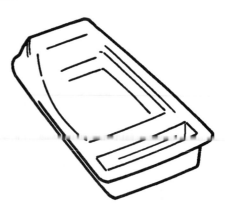

962 Laundry Tub

Cut the legs off of an old laundry tub so that the tub is the desired height. Stand the tub on the floor. Plug the hole with a stopper and fill the tub with water. Let two to four children at a time play with water toys in the tub.

963 Sink

Fill a sink with water. Set a stool in front of the sink. Let the children take turns standing on the stool and playing in the water.

Water Table Props

964 Basic Water Table Props

Set out a variety of the items listed below for the children to play and experiment with at the water table.

- balloons filled with water
- basters
- blown-up balloons
- bowls
- clear-plastic containers
- dish mops
- dishpans
- eyedroppers
- funnels
- marbles
- margarine tubs
- measuring cups
- measuring spoons
- paintbrushes
- Ping-Pong balls
- pitchers
- plastic containers
- plastic tubing
- scoops
- sieves
- sponges
- spoons
- spray bottles
- straws
- rotary eggbeaters
- whisks

965 Bubble Blowers

Show the children how to operate the following props under water to create bubbles.

- basters
- dishwashing liquid bottle
- plastic straws
- plastic tubing

966 Bubbles

Add a few drops of dishwashing detergent to the water in the water table. Show the children how to use a rotary eggbeater, a whisk or their hands to stir up bubbles.

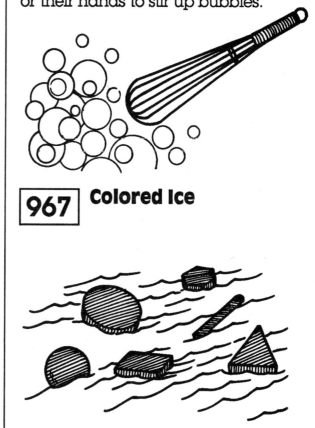

967 Colored Ice

Fill plastic containers and molds with water. Add different shades of food coloring to each container and freeze. Put the colored ice in the water table.

968 Floaters

Let the children experiment with floating the following objects on water.

- blown-up balloons
- corks
- metal lids
- pieces of wood
- Ping-Pong balls
- plastic animals
- plastic boats
- plastic containers
- plastic dishes
- plastic foam food trays
- plastic lids
- plastic straws
- plastic toys
- sponges

969 Ice Sculptures

Fill freezer-safe containers such as empty cardboard milk cartons, frozen pop molds, ice cube trays and plastic containers with water and place them in the freezer. Remove the ice shapes from the containers and place them in the water table.

970 Plastic Bottle Funnel

Cut the bottom off of a plastic bleach or soft-drink bottle and smooth out any rough edges. Clean and rinse out the bottle. Let the children use the top of the bottle as a funnel.

971 Shower Bottle

Cut the bottom off of a baby powder container and fill it with water. Let the children open and close the top of the container to make showers in the water table.

972 Sinkers

Let the children experiment with the following items that sink.

- bars of soap (not Ivory)
- marbles
- metal toy cars
- plastic containers filled with water
- rocks
- spoons

973 Snow

Fill the water table with snow. Have the children wear mittens while playing in it.

974 Soup Can Sprayer

Clean and rinse an empty soup can. Make sure there are no sharp edges around the rim. Punch holes in a vertical line from the top to the bottom of the can. Let the children fill the can with water and watch it spray into the water table. Have them observe the water spraying farther from the bottom holes.

975 Sponge Bucket

Place a variety of colors and sizes of sponges in a bucket. Place the bucket near the water table. To make the sponges more fun to play with, cut them into shapes such as animals, people, boats, flowers, etc.

976 Sprinkler

Clean and rinse an empty soup can. Punch holes around the bottom of the can, about one inch up. Have the children fill the can with water and watch it sprinkle out.

977 Warm Water

Put warm water in the water table and let the children play in it. Add more warm water as necessary to keep the desired temperature.

978 Water Carriers

Set out objects such as the following for the children to use to hold and carry water at the water table.

- canteens
- dishpans
- ice cube trays
- ladles
- measuring cups
- plastic containers
- small pitchers
- teapots
- watering cans

979 Water Squirters

Let the children use the following objects to carefully squirt water at the water table.

- basters
- dishwashing liquid bottles
- liquid soap dispensers
- spray bottles with pumps
- spray bottles with triggers

Water Toys

980 Colorful Water Bottle

Fill a jar or bottle (a plastic soft-drink bottle works well) halfway with water. Drop some shavings from crayons into the water. Let the children take turns shaking the bottle and watching the shavings create designs as they float to the top of the water.

981 Fish In the Bottle

Fill a clear-plastic 2-liter bottle one-quarter full with water. Add a few drops of blue food coloring. Blow up two small balloons, release most of the air and tie the ends closed. Push the balloons into the bottle. Put glue around the rim of the bottle and screw the cap on tightly. Let a child hold the bottle on its side and gently rock it back and forth to make the balloon "fish" swim.

982 Water Table Barge

Use the colorful water bottle from prop 980 as a colorful barge in the water table.

983 Wave Machine

Fill a small glass or plastic jar two-thirds full with water. Add a couple of drops of blue food coloring and mix well. Then fill up the rest of the jar with mineral oil, getting rid of as many air bubbles as possible. Secure the lid. Let the children hold the bottle sideways and gently tip it to create "waves."

Writing Props

984 Bread Dough

Let the children form alphabet letters out of bread or pretzel dough. Then bake the letters according to your recipe directions.

985 Brushes And Water

Take the children outdoors on a sunny day. Give them each a small paintbrush and provide buckets of water. Let the children dip the brushes into the water and paint lines or letters on a fence, an outside wall, a sidewalk, a picnic table or any other appropriate surface.

986 Carbon Paper

Assemble typing paper, carbon paper and paper clips. Make a "tablet" for each child by stapling together two sheets of typing paper with a piece of carbon paper in between. Place the tablets on a table, making sure that the shiny sides of the carbon papers are facing down. Let the children use large pencils to write letters on the top sheets of their tablets. Then have them lift their carbon papers to reveal the letter prints they have created on their bottom sheets.

987 Chalk

Take the children outdoors and let them write on a sidewalk or other paved surface with large pieces of chalk. To help develop large muscle coordination, have the children make basic strokes while moving their entire arms rather than just their hands and fingers. Wash away the chalk marks with a garden hose.

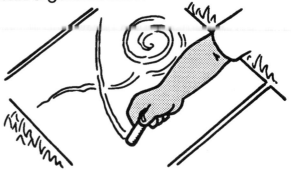

988 Chalkboard Writing

Let the children use wet brushes to create freehand letters on a chalkboard just after it has been erased.

989 Erasable Tablet

Purchase an erasable tablet that comes with a small writing stick (available at variety and toy stores). Let one child at a time practice drawing letters on the tablet. Have the child raise the top writing sheet to erase the drawings.

990 Fingerpaint

Encourage the children to try making different alphabet letters while they are fingerpainting. If desired, use your finger to draw letters on the children's papers for them to trace over or copy. Have the children smooth out the paint when they are ready to try making new letters.

991 Flashlights

Print extra-large letters on a chalkboard or on pieces of butcher paper attached to a wall. Give the children lighted flashlights and darken the room. Let the children trace over the letters on the chalkboard or wall with the beams of their flashlights.

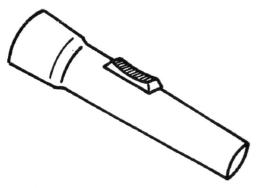

992 Glue

Have the children place pieces of construction paper inside large box lids. Give them small bottles of white liquid glue. Let them squeeze the glue onto their papers to create lines, shapes or letters. Then have them sprinkle sand or glitter on top of the glue and tap off the excess into the box lids.

993 Noodles

Break dried spaghetti noodles in half and cook them according to the package directions. Drain the noodles and allow them to cool. Give each child a piece of waxed paper and some of the wet spaghetti. Let the children use the noodles to form different alphabet letters on their papers. If desired, conclude the activity by helping the children form the letters that spell their names. When the letters have dried, they can be glued on sheets of dark colored construction paper.

994 Playdough

Give the children lumps of playdough. Have them roll the dough into long snakes. Then show them how the snakes can be twisted and turned to form different letters.

995 Salt Box

Cut black paper to fit inside the bottom of a sturdy shallow box and attach it in place. Cover the bottom of the box with a thin layer of salt. Let the children take turns drawing letters in the salt with their fingers. Show them how to erase their letters by gently shaking the box from side to side.

996 Sandpaper

Cut large letter shapes out of sandpaper. Glue the letters on heavy cardboard squares. Then let the children take turns tracing over the sandpaper letters with pieces of chalk.

997 Self-Stick Paper

For each child print letters, short words or the child's name on a separate piece of lined writing paper. Cover the papers with clear self-stick paper. Let the children practice tracing over the letters or words on their papers with black crayons. To erase the crayon marks, wipe the surface of the papers with a dry tissue or cloth.

998 Shaving Cream

Place small puffs of shaving cream on cookie sheets, plain plastic trays or a washable tabletop. Let the children spread out the shaving cream with their hands and enjoy finger-painting with it. Then show them how to use their pointer fingers to draw letters in the shaving cream.

999 Slates

Use chalk to print letters on a small chalk slate and let the children trace over them with their fingers.

1000 Snow

Just after a snowfall, help the children bundle up and take them outdoors. Look around for a patch of snow that is clear and unbroken. Give the children tongue depressors or other kinds of safe sticks. Then let them draw lines or letters in the snow.

1001 Soap Crayons

Purchase boxes of soap crayons (available at many bath stores). Let the children use the crayons to write on the bottom and sides of a dry sink or bathtub or on any other similar surface. To erase the crayon marks, wipe them with a wet sponge or cloth.

A

Materials Index